LIFE:
CHALLENGES AND SOLUTIONS

Divaldo Franco
by the Spirit Joanna de Ângelis

Life:
Challenges and Solutions

LEAL Publisher

ISBN: 978-1-942408-52-9

Original title in Portuguese:
VIDA: Desafios e Soluções
(Brazil, 1997)

Translated by: Darrel W. Kimble and Claudia Dealmeida
Cover design by: Cláudio Urpia
Layout: Luciano Carneiro Holanda
Edited by: Evelyn Yuri Furuta

Edition of
LEAL PUBLISHER
8425 Biscayne Blvd. Suite 104
Miami, Florida 33138, USA
www.lealpublisher.com
info@lealpublisher.com
(305) 306-6447

Authorized edition by Centro Espírita Caminho da Redenção – Salvador (BA) – Brazil

INTERNATIONAL DATA FOR CATALOGING IN PUBLICATION (ICP)

f825   Ângelis, de Joanna (Spirit).
       Life: Challenges and Solutions / authored by the Spirit Joanna de Ângelis; psychographed by Divaldo Pereira Franco ; translated by Darrel Kimble and Claudia Dealmeida. – Miami (FL), USA : Leal Publisher, 2014.
       155 p. ; 21 cm

       Original title: VIDA: Desafios e Soluções

       ISBN 978-1-942408-52-9

       1. Spiritism. 2. Psychology. 3. Behavior
       I. Franco, Divaldo Pereira, 1927-. II. Title.
                       CDD 133.9
                       CDU 133.7

CONTENTS

THE MIRACLE OF LIFE

*A*s much as the human mind asks questions about life in the conjuncture of today's undeniably vast intellectual knowledge, it is still difficult to find adequate answers that enable it to grasp life's full meaning and significance.

Some researchers have simplified life by reducing it to the absurdity of chance occurrences devoid of any logic whatsoever, thereby doing away with any further concern about its magnitude. Due to components of the supernatural and extraordinary, others have established it on easily acceptable mythological bases.

*But the **miracle of life** is much more complex than that, and for that very reason, its point of origin can only be found in the Creator, who engendered it and who has been guiding it across billions of years, effecting indispensable adaptations, developments and variations in its structure...*

*Regarding human life in particular, we can detect its genesis in the Divine Psyche, which conceived it and inspires it, providing it the energy with which it is nourished, which, in turn, drives its growth through the multifarious reincarnations of the immortal spirit, also called the **intelligent principle of the Universe**. **Simple** in its constitution, this intelligent principle liberates the complexities necessary for its growth, like* *a seed that becomes swollen in the benevolent heart of the soil in order to become the plant that it is meant to be, but which lies sleeping within.*

__Ignorant__ about its destiny, the immortal spirit awakens to its own reality by means of intellectual and moral experiences that enable it to achieve plenitude.

Like the humble yet noble seed which, due to its __death__, will never behold the golden ear that emerged from it, the spirit, in its initial simplicity as a psyche, cannot perceive the pure spirit that lies silent in its inner being, and which one day will sail the infinite __rivers of Immortality__.

This process of evolution, however, is characterized by challenges that become increasingly serious and significant as the spirit's faculties and discernment develop.

The blooming of inner values is, in a certain way, agonizing in all living species.

Plant life breaks through the seed's protective husk in order to free itself; the same occurs with human beings, who, at the start, find themselves enveloped by the strong carapace that incarcerates them. This prison leaves deep marks that must be eliminated as they continue to develop and begin to aspire to vaster realms and a more glorious destiny.

Their struggle, therefore, becomes intense and relentless, intensifying according to their capacity for endurance and enlightenment, which make victory possible.

Living is a sublime challenge, and living wisely is a blessing that is available to all who resolve decidedly to advance, overcome personal limitations and attain communion with God.

In this modest book, we shall study a few of the different challenges that modern men and women face in their daily lives.

Thanks to the invaluable endeavors of the different psychological approaches in general and that of Spiritist psychology in particular, excellent contributions have been put forth and are available to all those who are sincerely interested in constructing a sound conscience, a lucid and responsible individual, and a thriving society.

We are not presenting some magic formula – there is no such thing – that can resolve the natural difficulties and problems that are part of the process of evolution.

All proposals and solutions to the existential challenges of life depend on the effort, perseverance and confident action of each person.

Whatever cannot be achieved at one moment through wholesome persistence will be achieved at a later time.

We acknowledge the fact that there are excellent Works that address some, if not nearly all, of the topics contained in this book, and with better contributions.

Our humble collaboration, however, is founded on the powerful postulates of the Spiritist Doctrine, which, with the publication of **The Spirits' Book** *by Allan Kardec[1] on April 18, 1857, has been illuminating lives and liberating consciences for almost 140 years.[2]*

We trust that, albeit inexpressive, our offering may help readers faced with challenges discover solutions and become harmonized on their journey to happiness.

JOANNA DE ÂNGELIS
Salvador, Brazil, January 20, 1997

---

[1]   (1804-1869) The Codifier of Spiritism – Tr.

[2]   This book was first published in Portuguese in 1997 – Tr.

Note by the Publisher of the Portuguese version – With the publication of this book, we are paying homage to *The Spirits' Book* by Allan Kardec on the 140th anniversary of its publication. Moreover, we are congratulating the medium Divaldo Pereira Franco for observing his 50th year of Spiritist labor entailing mediumistically induced lectures, initiated on March 27, 1947, in the city of Aracaju, Sergipe, Brazil.

1
LIFE

Definition and purpose. Natural, domestic, affective, social and economic impediments to personal interrelating. Sickness and health. Obsessions.

DEFINITION AND PURPOSE

Good lexicographers define life as: *A set of properties and qualities, by which animals and plants, unlike dead organisms or raw matter, are maintained in continuous activity manifested as organic functions such as metabolism, growth, reaction to stimuli, adaptation to the environment, and reproduction.*[3]

Life may also be seen as the period that elapses between the actions and reactions that vitalize living beings as a result of highly complex cellular organizations, which develop between birth and death.

In spite of the absence of fossil remains – which have certainly disappeared rather than having never existed – it is believed that life began during the Precambrian Era, since in the subsequent Cambrian the presence of rich and diversified fauna was already voluminous.

---

[3] Free translation of the definition by the Spirit Author, from the Portuguese dictionary, *Dicionário Aurélio* – Tr.

Whenever there is a cellular structure, there is a living being. In the case of viruses, some of them do not yet possess a cellular structure and thus cannot be regarded as such.

All living beings depend largely on the consumption of energy that reaches earth through the light of the sun, converting 420 million metric tons of mass per second to maintain the solar system and, consequently, all life forms on our planet, especially plants, which serve as a foundation for maintaining the vegetables alongside other substances, which, in turn, nourish the animals.

Despite these various expressions for understanding life, it transcends the limits imposed by the deficiency of language, the poverty of form and the manner of understanding its profound meaning, which hides it even from the eyes of the most attentive observers.

Life manifests according to its own particular structure and may be discerned by each scholar or analyst, in accordance with his or her angle of understanding upon seeing and perceiving it.

St. Augustine defined it philosophically quite simply as *nutrition, growth and deterioration, caused by a principle that would, in itself, bring its own end,* which he called *entelechy.*

Claude Bernard considered it *impossible to define due to being inaccessible and abstract.*

Therefore, the definition of life varies according to the school of philosophical thought or scientific discipline, since individuals anchor their view of it on their respective foundations of cultural support.

Mechanists explain that life originated by means of purely physical-chemical phenomena. Vitalists believe in a *vital principle* that transforms lifeless matter into animated or pulsating matter. Dialectical materialism states that life must have originated in *a system in which everything changes, in an incessant movement of some parts superseding others; a system in which there are no isolated phenomena – everything is interrelated.*

Spiritualism starts from the reality of a Transcendent Being that created life and continues to maintain it, allowing for an infinite quantitative and qualitative development on its way to perfection.

Biologists state that life is the result of cells organized in remarkable agglutinations, forming individualized organs, systems and functions.

Philosophers offer various formulations that derive from their experiential and cultural perspective, in accordance with the School to which they belong; however, they restrict life to the period between the cradle and the grave.

Artists, according to their particular area of interest, attempt to translate life into beauty and majesty, copying it, manifesting it with either enchantment or disillusionment, depending on their individual psychological structure.

…And thus, successively, people understand and define life in accordance with their own perception, emotion and cultural capacity, furnishing concepts that are compatible with their own way of being.

At any given moment, however, life is an extraordinary chemist that transforms water and humus into wood and sugar in the plant, giving fragrance to the flower and flavor to the fruit, whereas in the stomach, it prepares powerful juices that break down food and digest it so that beings that are thus nourished do not die.

At the same time, life is an extraordinary artist that paints all the leaves of plants with rich contours that are never repeated, and endows each person with fingerprint patterns that are never found on another. Concomitantly, it uses its magical touch to give color and brilliance to plants, birds and all other living beings, while it adorns nature with enchanting festivals of infinite hues impossible to duplicate.

Life is an incomparable physicist that manipulates every energy field, enabling human beings to only gradually understand its *miracles*, now open to the countless areas of knowledge that fascinate the most astute minds.

Life arises from the joining of protoplasm and a ray of sunlight, which causes it to *split*, multiplying it to infinity – every living thing on earth began in this way. This fantastic joining of diaphanous energies is so powerful that the lowly root in an insignificant cranny can slowly culminate its development by splitting the rock apart...

In human beings, life is both fragile and powerful at the same time, in that it has structured the human body with resources that enable it to withstand varying atmospheric pressures and hard jolts, whereas, on the other hand, it could be affected by a tiny pinprick, which, having become infected, could cause death. It could also end due to a cut that led to blood loss because the fibrin clot did not form; or due to a minor trauma... An apparently ordinary bout of the flu or a viral disease can affect it gravely, whereas it naturally bounces back from serious infections, major surgeries and transplants. It can become sick or be healed under the command of the mind, the will, by receiving oxygen, water and, especially, love.

Life, however, is God, and is thus difficult if not impossible to be fully understood beyond its manifestations, which make up part of beings' reality, preceding their appearance in material form and continuing after their bodily decomposition.

In the incomparable and non-dimensional ocean of Life, we live under Laws that have set the essential guidelines for the happiness awaiting everyone, and which is the exceptional destiny for which Life manifests in the world: perfection!

NATURAL, DOMESTIC, AFFECTIVE, SOCIAL AND ECONOMIC. IMPEDIMENTS TO PERSONAL INTERRELATING

In studying the primordial beginnings of planet Earth, one can imagine the serious impediments to the appearance of life.

Extremely high temperatures, incessant geological upheavals, poisonous gases hovering in the atmosphere, widespread turmoil on the verge of chaos...

Slowly, however, the psyche existing within the vast *primordial soup* that covered the earth descended into the midst of the abyssal waters of the oceans, giving rise to the first molecules, while, at the same time, appeasing the scorching heat and abating the enormous tidal waves smashing against the rocks.

Molecular agglutination had its beginning in obedience to an intelligent, complex and transcendental plan, and the *divine breath*, in the form of life, began to sustain initial organizations.

After nearly two billion years, human beings have turned their thoughts to conquering the macrocosm, sending out space probes that offer them a much deeper understanding of the solar system, and they advance audaciously on a course much farther than their own orbit...

However, moral growth has not kept pace with this technological development, and, consequentially, human beings themselves are a threat to the very ecosystem that safeguards their physical life. They have become crazed by frantic ambition and have dived headlong into the abyss of maddening pleasure...

But of course, life triumphs over its hostile environment and hundreds of thousands of species appear, develop and vanish in 100,000-year (approximately) cycles.

The evolution of the forms that envelop the psyche, the growth of aspirations, and the grasping of progressively higher values, all which beacon the intelligence and sentiments to the never-ending endeavor of sublimation, are inexorable.

In the sequence of the cycles of evolution, the gains and losses of each lifetime are inevitably reflected in the next one, requiring individuals to make a greater effort to purify and develop other latent aspects waiting for an opportunity.

Therein reside other impediments to the expression of life, impediments of a domestic, social, affective, economic and interpersonal nature.

Hence, on account of its own actions the spirit repeats, due to automatic atavisms, the same experiences, particularly those in which it failed, until it learns better ways.

Aristotle stated that *knowledge is acquired and virtue is practiced* so that wisdom may be gained.

The knowledge of duty and the virtue of responsibility walk side by side, developing and perfecting latent resources, thanks to the contributions of successive reincarnations.

In light of this conjuncture, domestic or family impediments are rooted in the need of the *intelligent principle* – which governs human life – to live with the problems or blessings it caused in previous endeavors, to whose roots it remains connected.

Problem homes, frictional family relationships, the presence of a dominating mother and an authoritarian father, fomenting the appearance of conflicts in the child's personality, go back to past lifetimes entailing irrationality, instinct and intemperance.

When parents are finally convinced that the home is a sanctuary for human life and not a battleground for the supremacy of the ego; when adults become aware that education is an act of love and not a means of intimidation, of problem dumping; when people understand the family as being a dignifying commitment and not a boxing ring, then the tragic incidences of child abuse by violence, indifference and rape, and by the misery into which individuals are born and to which they are relegated, will give way to a just, equitable and happy society. Mistreated children, from whatever aspect, project onto society the specter of their oppressive fear and heartrending neglect, and at the first opportunity they will try to use cruelty to exact the love that has been denied them.

If one were to investigate the social origins of hardened criminals, except for those of a pathological nature – heredity, impairment due to obsession – one would find unhappy homes, dysfunctional families or perverse groups brought together in family simulacra, suffering the abuse and neglect of unconscionable and small-minded persons, or by even more insensitive systems, which collapse due to the very heinousness of the laws that support them.

Family impediments can be overcome with a love consciousness, understanding the circumstances of reincarnation and managing conflicts by means of specialized therapies and support groups.

Affective impediments result from many factors, including those stemming from individuals' emotional dysfunctions: timidity, inferiority and superiority complexes, narcissism...

Unhealed, perturbing *psychological scars* cause them to seek refuge in their unhappy childhood as they strive to sustain the low self-esteem with which they are engrained or stereotyped, thereby denying themselves the freedom and the right to be happy.

Deprived of love and thus unable to develop it, these individuals yearn for the very affection they fear. They are afraid to love and do not believe they are deserving of any sort of affection, and in their insecurity they develop jealousy, systematic distrust, and control over others, or they experience deeper psychological traumas that end in crime when they extinguish the physical life of the one they passionately love or the one who loves them.

In the immense gamut of perturbing conflicts, such individuals dissociate from social life, at first through a fragmentation of the personality, which feels shattered, slipping into either self-pity or aggressiveness, depending on their psychological makeup. It is inevitable that, in such a distressing situation, social life becomes unbearable or exerts a type of stressful emotional pressure, a fact that pushes them toward alienation. At times, fearing the invasion of its privacy, which acts as a self-defense mechanism, the social group is closed – an impediment to growth – and it prevents new members from joining. This is characteristic of the early evolutionary stages. Nevertheless, many times it is the insecure, tormented individuals themselves who reject society, hiding behind the excuse that they would not be accepted even if they did insist and even if they did overcome their limits and resistances.

The self-preservation mechanism is always present whenever there are conflicted personalities regarding social behavior: avoiding the group, yet accusing it of rejection.

On the other hand, financial problems generate impediments to existential coming to plenitude because they foster economic inferiority complexes in the midst of seemingly thriving people who strut their success, health and happiness…

It is known that wealth certainly does help individuals and their social group to advance; however, under no circumstances can it keep them from experiencing all the sufferings that are common to everyone else. It may mitigate difficulties, lessen some trials and afford personal comfort, but it can never impede the ordeals that affect everyone, especially inner ordeals, which precede current behavior.

When one has a structured personality, economic challenges do appear but they are evaluated so that they may be overcome; thus, a level of balance is achieved. Such challenges in no way invalidate the real values that adorn every person's inherent character. Consequently, it is not whether or not one has financial/economic resources, but the way one faces the situation, or the degree of one's psychological dependence in relation to the challenging circumstance.

The way all, some, or just one of these impediments perturb social interrelating depends on each person's emotional structure.

A well-developed and unhindered personality sees challenges and existential impediments as tests of its character. It feels invited to engage in struggles and endeavors that further develop its ability to confront future difficulties. Psychological maturity occurs little by little, and never because of a sudden event, much to the liking of the insecure and dreamers.

As long as the impediments to reaching the plenitude of life are identified, the individual experiences growth, in a process of existential valorization, of intellectual/moral development. Instead of being seen as obstacles, impediments should be seen as stimuli, as a dare for discovering and applying unknown resources that may be used effectively for personal harmony.

Sickness and Health

Health is the ideal state in life. Sickness is a perturbing vibrational occurrence, a change of behavior in the individual's molecular organization or in his or her still-maturing psyche.

This dystonia in the individual's most-delicate physical inner workings, which opens the way for the manifestation and proliferation of degenerative disorders, is seated in the intricate fabric of the spirit, which is heir to the acts that accompany it along its lengthy evolutionary journey. The spirit is always responsible for what it is and for what it sets out to do.

Sickness, however, is not always a state of calamity in the organic machinery or in the mechanisms responsible for the expressions of the intelligence, thought and emotions. When well-understood and directed toward higher purposes – achieved through careful thought and the maturation of ideas – sickness may, in many cases, be seen as preventative therapy against even worse ills – those of a profound moral nature and spiritual significance – a reminder that the somatic organization is always a garb of brief duration, and that the Self[4] per se is what deserves the full investment of concern and illuminative, self-preserving effort.

Life's destiny establishes balance, harmony and perfection, for individuals are rebellious or careless, and thus go through stages of maladjustment that open the way for the onset of diseases.

Health results from a good dose of psychological values that are in consonance with physical stability and emotional order, which produce a *climate* of vitality suitable for the functioning of the body. Any alteration in the delicate components of the physio-mental machinery readily provides the propitious conditions for the emergence of sickness. In this way, the psyche bears a great responsibility, in that, thanks to its frequency – in charge of maintaining perfect interplay between the physical, emotional and mental aspects – the events in these different areas may suffer alteration.

---

[4] The totality of the psyche, according to C.G. Jung – Tr.

A sound psychological education – the result of striving to cultivate spiritually uplifting ideas – is of major significance to a healthy life, responsible for future physical and psychological behaviors that always produce well-being and happiness. The same occurs when perturbing mental habits take root producing emotional distress, a physical field vulnerable to the invasion of degenerative microbial agents, and psychical grief, which are passed down from one incarnation to the next as the result of the *Law of Cause and Effect*.

Therefore, every effort to safeguard the mind against the intrusion of ideas bearing destabilizing energies acts as preventative psychotherapy, responsible for a healthy life.

OBSESSIONS

Every undue mental and emotional fixation regarding persons, facts and things becomes a perturbing behavioral state that pushes the individual toward neurotic and psychotic disorders.

Such instances may precede the current lifetime or they may appear during the present one as a result of unbridled ambition, behavioral excesses or exaggerated cravings that affect the *brain's metabolism*, fostering a decompensation in the production of the enzymes that affect the harmony of one's nervous system in general and one's behavior in particular.

As they become the dominant idea, they turn into obsessions that begin to trouble the individual, leading him or her to more serious states in the area of mental health.

Thus, compulsive obsessions arise, states of fragmented personality on the verge of behavioral degeneration. At other times, obsessions are phenomena that proceed from other lifetimes in which the spirit failed, being the object of profound conflicts or aggressive circumstances that damaged its perispiritual[5] structure, now responsible for the pathological condition.

Along the same lines, due to having been the object of dreadful wrongs in the ethical, moral, mental or behavioral arena, certain spirits now tune in to those responsible for their misfortune, and despite living in another dimension, i.e. the spirit realm, they begin persecuting them either subtly or violently in the realm of the mind. This gives rise to other types of obsession: those of spiritual origin, made possible by the presence of mediumistic faculties in patients, who begin to suffer highly diverse constraints until they fall into the abysses of madness, outrageous behavior and mental alienation.

The conscience cannot be evaded. It is the battlefield where the struggles for rehabilitation or the clashes for the regularization of unwholesome attitudes are fought.

Thus, mental control and thought education may still prove to be an effective therapy for the prevention of disturbances, or as the healer for processes of a spiritual order, if individuals would change the bandwidth along which their ideas travel. When such ideas are of a superior nature, individuals ascend and thus become immune to attunement with less-evolved beings. However, when they are negative, individuals begin to comingle on levels where

---

[5] From the word "perispirit": Kardec's terminology for what is also known as the astral body – Tr.

energies conflict and clash, and sentiments are in a constant struggle; they absorb such toxic emissions, which ultimately end up affecting the physical body and the complex mental components responsible for health.

The obsessions that result from psychological traumas, profound conflicts, and insufficient, specific, neuronal enzymes, also arise due to interference from the minds of discarnate beings, who, in perverse dynamics of revenge, act on those to whom they are directed.

Health requires specific care that can and must be had in order to keep it unaltered. Should it become affected, medical and spiritual guidance must be implemented so that it may accomplish its duty: to help the incarnate spirit on its cellular, temporary journey toward plenitude. This plenitude may be foreseen on the earth but can only be enjoyed once the present reincarnation is over, when the bodily mechanisms subject to the degenerative process of matter are no longer at the mercy of their inherent fragility and the imperatives of the law of entropy.

2
MEANING OF THE EXISTENTIAL BEING

Objectives of Human Life. Personal Conflicts. Myths, Illusion and Reality.

OBJECTIVES OF HUMAN LIFE

No one would reincarnate on the earth if physical existence did not have a higher purpose. The individual is the product of a lengthy process of developing the infinite qualities that lie latent awaiting propitious means for their manifestation. Little by little, step-by-step, progress is made and solidified through habits that are incorporated into the individuality, which is the sum total of all the experiences accumulated through multifarious reincarnations.

Failures and successes are means for developing the conscience for the grandest achievements of its destiny, which is of a cosmic nature if attuned to the designs and plans of the universe.

As the *intelligent principle* passes through various levels of the evolutionary process, it solidifies all the experiences that comprise its patrimony of mental and moral growth, traversing the more difficult and labor-intensive periods of the initial phase in order to reach the levels of lucidity that enable it to comprehend and live according to the Sovereign Codes governing the cosmos.

During human beings' *primary thought* phase, all progress is made by means of instinctual automatisms, guaranteeing the fundamental biological functions so that they may develop discernment under the yoke of harsh work – a burden that becomes lighter as a result of their own efforts to evolve. In these primitive beings, hope sings about the expectations of future glory. They look up at the starry canopy but do not understand those *magical lights* blinking from afar, lights that seem to be close at hand.

The saga of evolution is long and at times painful, leaving deep furrows, which in other phases, under the unexpected stimuli of suffering, resurface in the form of inexplicable anguish or violence, desperation or heartbreak. These would become *archetypes*, exerting a powerful influence on individuals' psychological behavior across many corporeal existences, characterizing their upward progress. In each personality, with each incarnation, the archetypes get mixed in, giving rise to a number of parasitical and perturbing personifications that comprise the chapter of *multiple personalities*, which manifest as alienated behaviors. Psychological evolution is also anthropological evolution, especially in the early stages.

Advancing slowly yet surely, learning from the *living forces* of the universe, individuals store up invaluable resources of knowledge that has cost them innumerable sacrifices on the long road of experience, and they now question themselves about the purpose of that entire pathway of growth. Finally, they discover that they are on the threshold of truly fulfilling and profound accomplishments, for they mean deliverance from residual atavisms, raising the aspirations to a realm of purer, thus less-anguishing, emotions, that is, those that do not result in weariness, bitterness or discouragement.

Individuals are predestined for happiness, for conquest of the Infinite beyond the expressions of space.

The suffering that oppresses them today is the hammer that prompts them to exit the situation that feeds the dysfunction.

At long last, as they comprehend the grandeur of love, they devote themselves to working for the general good, and they strive to master themselves, their neighbor and life in general. Everything that pulsates and vibrates interests them, delivers them from pettiness and leads them to greatness, shaping their inner being, which expands and harmonizes itself in a hymn of solidarity with everything and everyone, thus becoming an integral part of Life.

Existential meaning is discovered only when they reach a high degree of perception of reality, a reality that transcends the boundaries of the physical, transitory and experiential form, which, however, can and must be nourished with joy and complete health.

Therefore, one ought not mistakenly believe that the primary purpose of the existential experience is living the good life, that is, amassing wealth, enjoying amenities, finding pleasure in sensations that are renewed and then exhausted, making it to the winner's circle, and all such longings of *magical thought*, pursuing miraculous privileges and regalia that do not put individuals in harmony with themselves.

Of course, on the list of objectives and existential meaning are social, economic, artistic, cultural and religious accomplishments – all those that make up the world of interpersonal relationships. However, these are not exclusive, for they are not the end goals of one's searches and struggles, since individuals cross the threshold of the grave and continue to live, bringing along their plans for ascension engraved in their innermost being.

Struggling, within reason, for as much self-mastery as possible, facing challenges joyously, and grasping the fact that these are rungs on the ladder of ascension – this is how to incorporate into daily life the essential objectives of the physical, emotional and mental perfecting process.

Personal Conflicts

In the unavoidable endeavor of ascension, individuals must face the constructions of their past. These constructions are engraved within them and often manifest outwardly as afflictions and limitations, and inwardly as conflicts on the inner landscape. They threaten attempts at self-realization, the joy of work, and harmonious coexistence with others, easily becoming perturbing *complexes* in the realms of emotion and behavior.

The factors responsible for such disturbances cannot be denied. They start with the expectant mother's behaviors, which affect the fetus during its intra-uterine life, and they culminate with familial coexistence, particularly with domineering fathers and emasculating, neurotic mothers, who pass their insecurities and all their other problems on to their growing children, who, in turn, become debilitated under the heavy burden of tensions they are forced to bear. On the other hand, social, economic, cultural and educational pressures become terrifying giants that persistently persecute the student, who absorbs but cannot *digest* such ghosts; consequently he or she fears, detests and endures them throughout his or her life unless appropriate treatment is received. Of course, the spirit reincarnates in the place that is best for its evolution. However, since no one reincarnates to suffer, but rather to make reparation, acquire new experiences, develop aptitudes and grow inwardly, all the obstacles that individuals face are part of their educational plan; consequently, they must equip themselves with values and discernment in order to surmount them, and, freed from all restrictions on their liberty, advance confidently on their quest for self-fulfillment.

This is, above all, the function of psychology: to penetrate the core of individuals in order to unfetter them from the unfortunate conflicts and inheritances that weigh on their emotional economy.

Sigmund Freud – the eminent *Father of Psychology* – states with much personal correctness that *at the root of every neurotic conflict, there is always a problem of the libido*. One cannot discard the repressed manifestation of the libido concerning the various perturbing behaviors that affect human beings, because, leftover from their coeval experiences, individuals are reborn under the consequences of their past behaviors.

In the *Oedipus complex*, for example, we can see a reincarnational inheritance in which mother and son, in love with each other today, were husband and wife yesterday, when they made a shipwreck of their relationship. In the *Electra complex*, we see an ancestral coexistence between spouses or lovers, whom the Sovereign Laws of Life have brought together again in a different capacity, in order to overcome their previous connections of afflictive sexual conduct.

These reunited *lovers* bear in their unconscious, that is, in their spirit, the reminiscences of their tormented dynamics; they feel the appeals of yesterday reappearing vibrantly. And since they are devoid of strong morals, they plunge into an incestuous, and consequently unhappy, relationship.

Even in *inferiority* and *superiority complexes*, there is a resurgence of the dominating spiritual past, causing morbid states that lead to imbalance, one step away from mental alienation. We must not fail to mention familial, educational and social factors that contribute to the emergence of such perturbations, worsening distressing tendencies that deeply scar the psyche.

Regarding *phobias*, there are spirits that inwardly bear fears that have survived the biological event of reincarnation. These fears are scars left over from having lived in the *lower spirit realm*, or from having awakened in the grave while still alive and then having discarnated due to the lack of oxygen, consequently re-living their torment as *claustrophobia*. Likewise, memories of terrifying scenes, in which they participated in the crowd as either casualties or promoters , are unconsciously relived as *agoraphobia*.

In the various types of *depressive psychoses*, we must point out the presence of a *guilty conscience*, which pre-exists the body and, therefore, the current psychological structure, producing flight mechanisms in response to challenges, often under the control of neuronal enzymes responsible for the dysfunction, as well as proximate causal factors, and even spiritual obsessions, which play out in the *mental commerce* with human beings.

Along these lines, painful *compulsive obsessions* have their etiopathogenic roots in grave transgressions incurred by the spirit in past lives, marked by indifference toward human dignity or disrespect for established laws...

When the goal of education is the construction of the human being as a whole, causes of perturbation will give way to other types of stimuli that are builders of hope, supporters of lofty aspirations in the endeavor to overcome the unwholesome inheritances that each individual carries within.

MYTHS, ILLUSION AND REALITY

When children fail to mature psychologically after the *magical thought* developmental period, they transfer those constructions to every phase of their physical existence. They remain deceitful individuals, who seek refuge in *imaginative creativity* in order to avoid responsibility for their immature acts. This behavior is also deeply rooted in the *archetype* inherited from the ancestral human being, which went through the process of the evolution of thought and left the *marks* of that passage engraved in the collective unconscious.

However, the behavior of domineering parents, who feel compensated for a lack of love by their children's fawning and submissiveness, ensures that the mythical phase remains fixed in the structure of the infantile personality. Furthermore, they see their children as still-immature individuals, whom they would like to continue to guide, even after they have become adults. This is a conflict that is handed down from generation to generation, each time with more damaging results.

The lack of honesty in adults to analyze themselves and assume the courage to break free from all the impediments and bonds that keep them stuck in the past is responsible for such behaviors.

Inner insecurity is what makes dictators, who surround themselves with unjust laws, arbitrary acts, ruthless bodyguards and special treatment. They intimidate, destroy and make themselves hated in order to feel fulfilled. They believe that they can shift their own fears, regarding everything and everyone, onto the fear that others feel for them.

Myths, which are left over from the infantile period or the lack of maturity in the adult under the continued influence of specific archetypes, bring back to mind the old concepts about *gods, demigods, mages, fairies, ghosts* and *irrational beliefs* as ways of expecting divine protection involving superior deities, who arrive magically to save them from *human wickedness, unjust society, unfaithful friends…*

When they reach the age of reason, individuals' fear of their father is transferred to God, who reflects the detested image of their physical father, or to even more dreadful gods, conceived by their imagination in previous periods of a more primitive culture. Their arbitrary mother *constructs* in their unconscious the evil, jealous witch, to be defeated by the intercession of the fairy godmother. The conflicts of affectivity in the home fuel the hopes for a medieval-style romantic love, which will come to snatch the victim from his or her emotional dungeon of loneliness and dejection. Petty and perverse teachers, who find more pleasure in intimidating than in teaching, instill in their students' psyche the soulless invader who storms their existential castle to destroy it under the pretext of friendship and assistance.

Buried but not dead, *myths* are at the very foundation of the unconscious, always ready to assail the mental and psychological domains, leading individuals to take occasional flights by means of daydreams and fertile imaginations.

Life for such persons does have an aspect of complete reality; even so, all their aspirations are centered on the world of make-believe. They are positive that at any moment everything will change for them, and they will live happily ever after.

On account of this illusion, in which the physical life is everything, the essential purpose of existence causes terrible conflicts. Trusting with complete confidence in the material world, the very injunctions of personal development expose their structural fragility. This produces disenchantment, suffering and the breakdown of their ideals.

Belief based on the illusion that everything in the physical world is long-lasting, if not eternal, foments a clash with the reality of continuous transformation, which occurs due to the very transient nature of matter and everything clothed in it.

The essential being is resistant to human and environmental-related changes in its *habitat*. Constructed of thought energy, which is independent of the transitory nature of the somatic body, it pre-exists and survives it, thus being an ever-advancing reality that prevails over time and space.

The facts that prove this resist opposing theories and produce philosophical and psychological evidence to further establish its solidity.

The shift from illusion to reality is imperative for personal harmony and inner happiness.

Seeking the support of knowledge in order to discern what is illusory and what is real, what has a structure that endures time and cultural transformations and what is only enticement, offers an opportunity for psychological maturation and self-realization.

With this discernment, disruptive attachments, unjustifiable jealousies, the anguish of pointless anxieties and infantile disappointments due to the natural events of the evolutionary process give way to freedom from persons, things and pleasures, which, although a motivation for living, are not the sole purpose.

The events of birth, death, old age and sickness are inalienable realities because they are part of the mechanics of physical life. Making the days lived in the body more enjoyable, eliminating perturbing factors that, at times, make life unbearable, and basing one's knowledge on actual experience – these are options within the grasp of all lucid persons, who can get what they want through personal effort.

Prolonging one's physical existence is possible, although for obvious reasons it cannot be prolonged indefinitely. Since one's own death or the death of one's loved ones is inevitable, confronting it serenely is a sign of balance; one should be neither surprised nor embittered by it.

Accepting individuals as they are, eliminating the idea that they are perfect – *gods or demigods* in the pantheon of illusion – functions as a barometer for emotional stability regarding the reality of human life. Life should entail neither passion nor abandonment, but awareness of how to live well in relative, terrestrial time.

3
CAUSES OF INSECURITY

Cunning Individuals. The Need to Lie.
Pathological Affection. Ineffective Support.

CUNNING INDIVIDUALS

With variations, Greek mythologists say that the city of Corinth, under Sisyphus, was experiencing a drought and did not have enough water for its survival.[6]

To save the city and its people, this mythological king kept a veritable army of *assailants* who attacked unsuspecting travelers passing through the region.

Due to his cunningness, Sisyphus was always informed about local events and those on Mt. Olympus.

Through his network of spies, Sisyphus learned that the god Asopus was desperate. His daughter Aegina had vanished without a trace and he was offering wealth and fertility to whomever could provide information that would lead to the kidnapped girl.

---

[6] See our book *Desperte e Seja Feliz* [Awaken and Be Happy], Ch. 24: *Inteireza Moral* [Moral Integrity], Ed. LEAL – Spirit Auth. (Not yet translated into English (2015). – Tr.)

Sisyphus used his cunning and discovered the girl's whereabouts. He went to Asopus and promised to talk in exchange for the reward. Asopus agreed and Sisyphus revealed that it was Zeus who had kidnapped and imprisoned the girl.

The distraught father went to the supreme god and demanded that his daughter be handed over. Unable to deny this request, Zeus acquiesced on the condition that he be told who the informant was. Asopus revealed his source.

Zeus became furious and sent Death to look for Sisyphus.

The cunning king, who thought he had solved the problem of his people and kingdom – which now enjoyed water in abundance – faced a new challenge: the dreaded terminator of lives. However, deeming himself invincible due to his guile, when Death arrived, he praised her and honored her with a special necklace that he said had been reserved for such an occasion. However, Sisyphus requested the pleasure of putting it on her himself. Death was flattered and accepted the king's gesture. And this is how Sisyphus managed to seize Death – the necklace was actually a shackle in disguise. Death was thrown into prison and Sisyphus, having defeated Zeus, thought himself free and clear of any further complications.

Other gods, however, such as Cronos – ruler of the seas and Hades – and Ares – god of war and death – went to Zeus and complained bitterly. With Death's imprisonment, Hades was not being repopulated and wars had ceased. Hence, they demanded that Death be freed and Sisyphus be put on trial.

This time, Zeus sent Hermes, who boldly appeared before the cunning king to enforce the postponed journey.

Caught by surprise, the god-king asked permission to say goodbye to his wife, and when he did, he whispered in her ear that, after his death, his body was not to be entombed, because he planned to return. Then, Sisyphus readily went with Hermes to Zeus, who had gathered all on Olympus for the ambitious king's trial. Right before his sentencing, and in front of all the gods, Sisyphus asked Zeus to allow him to return to earth in order to have his body receive the honors owed to kings, especially those of mythological origin. Furthermore, as was plain to see, he was without his *eidolon* (perispiritual body); thus, it was crucial that he return to the earth.

The Sovereign granted his request, but the moment Sisyphus retook his body, he and his wife immediately fled Corinth to avoid Zeus's wrath.

He thus solved one problem but created another, much more serious one, which he would have to face later on.

Urged by the other gods to punish the runaway, Zeus answered: *"I shall send a god whom he cannot run from forever: Time."* And he said no more.

Sisyphus ran as long as he could, but was eventually overcome by old age and infirmities. Death came looking for him again.

Once more in Zeus's presence, he immediately heard the punishment for attempting to cheat the Laws and avoid Justice. He would have to push a boulder up a mountain and set it on its peak. To ensure that he never slowed down, an Erinys was appointed to prod him with a pitchfork every time he showed signs of exhaustion.

To this day – say the mythologists – Sisyphus keeps trying to reach the peak of the mountain, but whenever he gets close, the boulder slips from his grasp and rolls back down to the bottom, requiring him to repeat the mighty undertaking unsuccessfully, over and over…

The story is a real warning to those who consistently put off their responsibilities and realities, believing in their own cunning. All who act in this manner believe they are very smart, whereas everyone else is stupid or naive.

Actually, cunning is not an expression of intelligence, but of self-preservation and self-interest.

Every individual faces challenges in order to grow. Earthly life itself is an ongoing summons to effort. The best way to solve problems is to resolve them at their source and avoid putting them off, for they will return even more complicated. Whatever is not done today will be much more difficult tomorrow.

Whenever a problem is resolved badly, it either gives rise to another, or it returns even more challenging than before. Consequently, only correct attitudes based on honor and loyalty can finally resolve problems and disagreeable occurrences along the way.

Immature individuals always put off solutions, believing the illusion that circumstances will be better tomorrow than they are today. They avoid facing their conscience and responsibilities. Their victories are won by means of disloyalty and improper conduct. They smile as they deceive others, but they are only fooling themselves, because responsibility always boomerangs for proper adjustment.

Psychological maturation means that every activity should take place at the right moment and that every challenge be met as soon as it appears.

Self-pity in the face of problems and cunning in order to avoid them are both infantile dynamics that solve nothing.

A problem solved means one more step taken and a new challenge ahead – such is the human evolutionary constant.

THE NEED TO LIE

Vestiges of the mendacity phase linger in immature adults, causing them to continue to distort reality to please their senses, thoughtlessly creating vexing situations that make them and others suffer. Afterwards, free of what could have been the unfortunate consequences of their act, and even having promised themselves they would not yield to such vice again, they lie anyway, due to their conditioning.

Infantile insecurity is evident in individuals who refuse to grow, believing they attract attention with this troubling behavior.

Lying must be rejected under whatever form it may appear because of the moral harm it causes, for it leads to defamation, slander and a whole string of awful psychological and ethical dystonias in the social dynamic. Liars are doubtlessly sick individuals, yet they elicit contempt on account of their behavior. No one believes what they say even on the rare occasions when they actually do tell the truth. It is completely natural for them to change the content or presentation of the facts, which they reveal in an unreal way, hoping to manipulate persons with this despicable ruse.

The roots of lying are found in the dysfunctional, unstable home, where insecurity is covered up with values *conceived* by the child's imagination. Personality conflicts induce fantasy behavior in a neurotic flight from reality. This is a veritable burden for such patients, one they would rather not deal with. To them, things and events should always be rosy and fine. So, when that is not the case – which is normal – it scares them, and seems to threaten their tranquility. Consequently, they falsify the facts.

Distorting reality has become so widespread that the so-called *white lie* was created; that is, one that is meant to be bland, one that does no harm, at least intentionally, and is used for avoiding situations that might be unpleasant if the real facts were told.

But the face of truth is transparent and must never be hidden. Throughout humankind's history, the greatest lessons have always been presented poetically, simulated and veiled, in order to last over time and have their meaning interpreted according to the parameters of each age. This applies to the Vedanta, the Bible, the Zend Avesta and the Koran, to mention just a few great spiritual works, and to the literature of Homer, Virgil, Ovid, Horace and Dante.

Thus are the tales, the sutras, the parables, the sagas and the koans.

Regardless of form, the truth, lightly hidden, stands out in such narratives in order to help those who, listening to their authors, may grasp their meaning and pass them down to posterity, which has benefitted from them down through the millennia.

Individuals nearly always exhibit a psychological reaction against the truth. They want to hear it, but sugarcoated – as people say – that is, they want the real truth glossed over. Of course, truth must not be wielded like a whip, which is a neurotic behavior, imposing oneself with one's own truth, hurting another person and thus feeling victorious in a perturbing dynamic of false moral superiority. All who act this way have a serious, unconscious inferiority complex that manifests as authority and supervision over human weakness.

The truth must be spoken naturally, kindly, unpretentiously, without imposition, but also without being falsified, without losing the power of its content.

Liars make up excuses, covering their wrong and blaming others – who seem to never understand them – thus avoiding taking responsibility for their altered information.

Discipline and strict watchfulness in the art of speaking, seeking to strictly repeat what one has witnessed, and withholding one's personal opinion – which does not correspond to the facts – are of vital importance for successfully dealing with reality.

The therapy of good reading, of wholesome moral habits, without sentimentality or self-pity, produces good results and harmonizes the individual in what he or she thinks, sees, hears and says.

Therefore, there is no need to lie. When a lie is told, it is a sign of a behavioral disorder that needs to be corrected.

Buddhist philosophy, amongst other lofty teachings, points out seven factors or conditions of wholesome conduct, establishing ideal ways for acting rightly, of which we would mention only a few: right thinking, right talking, right acting...

Thus, it is in thought that planning takes place; hence one must think rightly and talk rightly in order to act rightly.

This is why family life must be a place of emotional security, of complete fulfillment, and not a dumping ground for bad moods and daily tensions.

A seven-year-old child asked her mother, a television professional, why she was always smiling on TV, but was always grumpy and grouchy at home. Surprised by this question, the mother said that she was paid to smile on television. In response, her loving daughter asked, "So how much would you like to be paid to smile at home too?"

Children are more than just reproductions of the body. They are attentive spirits, some of whom are needy, while others are mature enough to press on and build the world of tomorrow. Every bit of care given to them always yields good results.

PATHOLOGICAL AFFECTION

Among the perturbing behaviors, pathological affection is a highly relevant topic. It appears in emotionally dysfunctional individuals, who express themselves in an unbalanced way, creating even more anxiety, dissatisfaction and dysfunction.

Insecurity and a lack of affection normally produce unnatural, unstable behaviors that draw negative attention.

Confusing love with passion, such patients transfer their potential for failure to their partner, whose life they intend to control with various manipulations. They feel unworthy of love, so they try to win pity, sympathy and make themselves needed, isolating their loved one from other relationships and activities. Ever-present, they seek to become both servant and lover just a hand's reach away.

Their affection is selfish and insatiable, bordering on pathological jealously, which they claim to be a demonstration of love, although it destroys all spontaneity in the relationship. Even when they are loved, they find it hard to believe it and they accuse their partner of feeling only pity, as opposed to the all-consuming and profound kind of love they expect.

They crave exclusive devotion to the point of suffocating their partner, who loses his or her self-identity under the implacable yoke of the emotional leech.

When they do find someone, the relationship is doomed because they are always wanting more, which makes living with them unbearable and psychological self-destruction inevitable. Their manners are artificial; their sole concern is to surround their beloved one with wearisome displays that they claim are indicative of their devotion. They do not grasp the fact that the other person has his or her own, differing concerns and longings and may not always be willing to endure such suffocation.

People are born to be free, and for that very reason love is a liberating sentiment that provides peace and joy. When manifested through unreasonable demands, it wanes and dies. Love has an unlimited capacity for understanding and tolerance, for being open and honest; it never lessens when faced with difficulties, for it has the resources to eliminate impediments and misunderstandings.

A healthy relationship entails dialog, consistent behavior, loyalty and authenticity, such that the presence of the other person does not inhibit but pleases, filling space without invading it. The person does not even realize how important the other one is until he or she is no longer around. Then, the affective depth and real meaning of that loved one is truly felt.

When insecure persons show affection, it is troublesome and wearisome. The objects of their so-called love actually feel better when they are not around their emotional controllers, who regard all who might be fond of their partner as adversaries or competitors, enviers or hinderers of their wholeness and happiness.

The roots of such behavior lie in a lonely, mistreated childhood, which was lived amidst conflict. Such persons have carried over to the future the desire to dominate in order to have instead of a personal commitment to be.

In childhood, unloved children get attention by crying, misbehaving, and deceiving; in adulthood, they do so by disguising their thoughts and actions with the intellectual resources within their reach.

In these cases, the libido functions under mistaken stimuli, when such individuals go from a state of possession to one of loss; they become exasperated and desirous of the other, and willingly subject themselves to a humiliating, unpleasant situation, provided it attends to their desperate ego.

Those who behave in this way almost never relax. They are constantly suspicious and seeking proofs about what they imagine to be. Consequently, they are always demanding more sacrifices, patience and displays of love, without ever feeling satisfied.

Pathological affection requires careful therapy so that such patients may regain their lost tranquility and self-assurance, both vital for conflict-free love.

The more such persons try to ignore the fact that their behavior is irregular, the more difficult it is for them to co-exist with other people. This is especially the case for those who tend to play the victim, projecting their guilt onto other people.

The courage to acknowledge the urgency of the situation and take responsibility by seeking appropriate therapy is a significant first step in the healing process.

INEFFECTIVE SUPPORT

In an attempt to avoid reality, insecure patients living troubled lives often resort to support mechanisms in order not to face their own conscience. As a result, they experience behavioral problems, which they systematically vitalize due to their inability to tell right from wrong – the reason behind the pathology.

Always playing the victim is one of the characteristics. They take refuge in this ruse, looking for pity and justification for all their imbalances. Seemingly always misunderstood, making no effort to understand others or taking responsibility for their acts, they become tedious and wearisome.

At other times they go from victim to petty accuser, seeing only what pleases them as opposed to what really happens, thereby making their situation even worse.

They are greatly concerned about bringing misinformed adherents into their personal circle by using infantile or perverse means such as defamation, slander and gossip, if it will help them achieve their purposes.

Dissimulation is habitual: it varies from jovial or innocent to unhappy or bitter, depending on the circumstance and the objective in mind.

These patients resort to such ineffective means of support due to their emotionally undeveloped, infantile personality. They naively believe that since they lack the courage to face their circumstances, their existence has to be a realm of fantasy and unreality.

Psychologically mature individuals face challenges and overcome them in an unhurried, natural manner, trusting in their own growth and the resources they can use in their social coexistence. Whenever they feel weak, they stop, think and start over, striving to become stronger in their own struggle. They avoid running away from their situation, because that would do no good whatsoever.

On the other hand, immature individuals face neither themselves nor others. They utilize special mechanisms to avoid taking a stand, assuming responsibilities or honoring them. At other times, they readily assume responsibilities in order to put off decisions and solutions, but ultimately shift them over to someone else.

It will take much effort for such patients to break free from the tendency to resort to such ineffective and, therefore, perilous support, and decide to face situations even if it requires much effort and struggle. Whatever the situation, they will have to do the work. And so be it, provided they aim at success instead of shifting responsibility; now instead of tomorrow; at the truth and liberation rather than fantasy and illusion, which vanish, leaving them hanging, and in greater emotional and actual insecurity.

4
ENERGIES OF LIFE

Mental Habits. Frustrations and Dependencies.
Sensations and Emotions. The Inner Life.

MENTAL HABITS

Biological life per se is the result of harmoniously functioning automatisms, provided that the organic components remain in working order. Abiding by the cardiac rhythm and brain reactions, all the phenomena are repetitive and predictable in keeping with ancestral atavisms. Subject to mesological factors and food nutrients, life flows unaltered during the first period of physical existence, marching unrelentingly toward its developmental destiny.

Mental life begins with glimpses and perceptions as the spirit masters the brain's mechanisms, which decode the spirit's thought waves. From the initial, instinctive impulses all the way up to cosmic understanding and the full range of experience, the spirit opens the floodgates of communication in order to become logical, before reaching the final step, which is oneness with Divine Consciousness.

After having successfully passed through the initial stages to finally arrive at the moment of reason, humans carry mental habits deeply imprinted in the inner recesses of their intellectual learning experience. These mental habits will guide their conduct from then on, for all existential programming starts with thought.

This issue is of major relevance because thought involves commands concerning what must be accomplished and how to go about it. If individuals allow themselves to be led by primitive, habitual manifestations, the labors that keep them trapped in their present developmental stage are repeated over and over without positive results and without the moral qualities needed to reach new levels of the evolutionary process.

Since the guidelines for behavior lie in thought, thinking correctly is the biggest challenge for anyone who truly desires victory.

As a result of past experiences, thoughts of pain, anguish and pessimism are the ones that are the most deeply engrained due to their destabilizing power. These are the unconscious evocations that are foremost in the assault on the mental house of individuals in their daily lives.

Bound to the repetitive dynamics of suffering-laden behavior, they tend toward self-punishment, unknowingly fostering mental habits that cause conflicts and distress.

They construct and suffer the effects of the notion that everything will always end badly; consequently, they do not make an effort to ensure that their attempts to change will be crowned with success. Destructive concepts regarding people, things and events further increase the charge of heavy and toxic mental energy, which impedes a correct, honest and healthy outlook that would redress the corrupted will.

Naturally inclined to such pessimism, which is fed in the realm of thought, they establish negative patterns regarding situations and people. They do not change the way they think or act and, consequently, they live under the stigma of ill humor, negative insinuations and bad luck, where they seek shelter in order to avoid the struggle that is necessary for success. Their mental clichés overwhelm all notions of mental wholesomeness concerning life and other people, rendering their existence a psychological chaos due to their unwillingness to change their ways.

Since all expressions of evolution depend on thought, from whence they come, it is easy to think differently by replacing an incorrect thought with one that seems favorable. People may claim not to know the difference, but all they have to do is evaluate what comprises their crutch – the thing that sustains their dysfunction – and then proceed to a new endeavor of a different sort.

At first, inertia will ensure the repetition of the old pattern and will breed disbelief in the success of the new undertaking. In this case, they must persist and persevere, opening up new space in their corrupted mental field to plant the new seeds of optimism and hope in order to exit the unhealthy state. Right afterward, it is imperative that they begin to value everything around them and establish new patterns of comprehension, thus freeing themselves from their old negative-pessimistic constructs.

The new habit will be slowly instilled in the subconscious until it becomes an integral part of the behavior.

Thinking rightly or wrongly is a matter of habit. Every time there is a demeaning, negative, perverse or unjust thought, it must be immediately replaced with a dignified, positive, loving, trusting, and fair one. Subsequently, it must be further sustained by the force or wave of one's desire. That which is thought about certainly does become a reality. This is so because thinking and acting are terms of the same existential equation. Think first and then act, rather than act first and then regret it after having thought about it.

Lofty mental constructions – those that produce healthy habits – are renewable and grow in the individual. They originate in the spirit, which receives them from the Divine Thought, whence come all the forces of spiritual growth and complete fulfillment.

FRUSTRATIONS AND DEPENDENCIES

One is always in the present moment, which is one's decision-making instant. The past is irrecoverable – although reparable – and cannot, therefore, serve as a parameter, except to teach how not to repeat one's errors. Nothing can be recuperated in the area of past moral wrongs; however, if there is genuine interest, they can be corrected. Thus, it is counterproductive to long for what once was, to feel frustrated about unfulfilled expectations, or to be deeply regretful about one's failures. Such feelings cannot change past outcomes, but they can be reframed by acting differently, thereby changing future results. Consequently, one must forgive everything and everybody, including oneself. Regaining one's emotional composure, one can restart the task at the point where it went wrong.

Psychologically sound individuals do not dwell on memories, nor are they tormented by their own aspirations.

They are rooted in a fulfilling present, and all their endeavors aim at furthering their own development. These people are naturally and rationally confident about the future, without worry or anxiety, living fully at every moment of their day.

Unstable personalities, on the other hand, are easily frustrated due to a lack of persevering idealism concerning their self-realization. They are either too ambitious or completely uninspired; they allow themselves to be seized by melancholic states of their own creation, and do not make a competent effort to exit their bad situation.

Innumerable factors contribute to personal frustrations, such as: the conflicts of an unfulfilled libido, which causes unjustifiable fears or depression; an unsatisfactory family life, in which the images of grouchy, nagging parents create anxieties and a desire to flee the stressful predicament; self-realization issues due to a lack of initiative, or small failures that could be transformed into successes if only they would persevere; jealousy regarding other people's successes, often achieved with great effort, which such individuals0 refuse to put forth...

Every string of frustrations leads individuals to emotional dependency. They create taboos, search for amulets to counter their unlucky star, experiment with the supernatural, and look for magical solutions with which to turn challenges into victories.

This dependence is transferred from superstitious beliefs to other individuals, who must psychologically, physically and economically endure them, fix their problems and resolve their difficulties, which constantly multiply due to the absence of decision-making and reasoning needed for acting appropriately. Unable to find anyone willing to bear

Joanna de Ângelis / Divaldo Franco

such a heavy burden, they feel increasingly frustrated and degenerate into a bipolar psychosis.

When individuals start considering the fact that they are on the earth at the right time, at the right place and with the right persons – those that are necessary for their evolution – they will awaken from their infantile dependency and debilitating frustration. They will regain behavioral health by means of mental renewal and enticing motivations that will render their existence more than just bearable – it will render it happy.

Individuals must aspire to the best, which, even if unattained, makes for an optimistic view to the future because it enables them to achieve what is achievable, without frustration or dependency regarding those who succeed.

Since thought is the source of aspirations, longing for what is best and working to acquire it represents moral elevation and growth. Not becoming upset when it is not attained, however, is a demonstration of maturity and balance, which all should maintain.

SENSATIONS AND EMOTIONS

Human beings are a bundle of sensations, as the natural result of their journey through the early periods of evolution, on their way to the reality of the emotions. Their extensive experiences in the primitive realms of the past left profound impressions that became a prevailing requirement in their personal, social and, especially, psychological behavior. Impulses and reactions make up part of this process, which establishes behavioral paradigms when outside the sieve of reason.

52

During that stage, emotional nourishment is received through objective sensations, through close contact with the world and its manifestations. As a result, they pursue an excessive game of wanting to have, rather than aspiring to be.

Asleep to the subtler perceptions of existence, they accumulate things and enjoy them to the saturation point; then they switch to possessing other persons, who may not consent to being so easily possessed. This causes emotional conflicts that disrupt the would-be possessors' intent. Frustrated because their desire does not translate into satisfaction, they become embittered and rebellious, and often turn to alcohol, tobacco or addictive drugs as an escape.

Change from the dense realm of immediacy to the subtleties of the higher emotions is very slow. During that journey it is normal to be confronted with the sensation-emotive phase, when there is a decompensation in the nervous system and excessive emotivity controls the behavior. Since they are not used to expressions of beauty, sincerity and love, they are easily moved and lose their balance. Nonetheless, this is the first step toward the harmonious environment awaiting them.

Sensation-seeking humans are demanding and possessive. They do not realize the value of other people's liberty, which they aim to control, nor are they aware of their duties toward society, which does not submit to them. Feeling marginalized due to the hostility they harbor toward all who do not bow to them, they turn against laws and free persons, becoming dehumanized and attacking others using every means possible.

But as their emotions awaken, they naturally value their neighbor and life, developing respect for human and overall values. At the same time, they start caring about progress and begin working for it, broadening their horizons of understanding and inner realization.

Sensation is the inheritance from the domineering instinct; emotion is the treasure to be gained on the roads of ascension.

When the conscience awakens to the need for emotion, the only alternative remaining is the struggle to attain it. This undertaking becomes easy when the battle begins, facilitating the encounter with its reality, that is, the thought energy that it is; it realizes it is not just a group of cells in specialized organs making up the body.

During the emotion phase, individuals are not free of sensations. Sensations continue to provide them with pleasures, joys and warnings, but they are under control, balanced, directed and productive. Likewise, in the sensation phase, individuals experience somewhat disordered emotions that at times provide them with well-being, which stimulates them to grow and make an effort to attain more of it.

In psychopathology there is a predominance of sensations and a major dysfunction of emotions, which is indicative of mental suffering reflected in alienated behavior.

We can find the roots of such a state in the dysfunctional home involving shortsighted, ambitious parents who are incapable of loving and who have taught their children that the only people that matter are those with possessions, whereas others exist just to serve them.

In essence, it is the still-developing spirit that reveals itself in the body, living stronger expressions in detriment to loftier ones.

Well-directed effort, the cultivation of ennobling ideas and edifying labor are of great help for all who aspire to stop lingering in the primitive phase and move on to the next level.

THE INNER LIFE

The cultivation of reflection, prayer and meditation are as necessary as physical nourishment for a healthy life. Physical nourishment meets the needs of the physical cells, whereas the other three meet the needs of those having to do with the psyche, i.e., generators of the material organization. Without harmonious vibrations coming from the psyche, the field where the cells of a congealed constitution are developed becomes imbalanced, and consequently dystonia in the *form* hampers the shaping on the outside.

Oxygen maintains the body, while the mental wave sustains life. Both are indispensable for a balanced individual, but these two resources are not always utilized wisely and properly. Some, understanding the need for proper breathing, pursue outdoor sports and recreation but ignore their inner life or other commitments essential to their real growth. Others, enchanted with the well-being they enjoy through the practice of inner disciplines, neglect human relationships and isolate themselves, bringing forth disintegrating factors in their behavior, which lead to selfishness and a lack of solidarity in the community.

A well-conducted inner life teaches individuals to accept themselves as they are, without wanting to imitate transitory models of momentary glories, which shine in the spotlight of illusion; and it also teaches them not to aspire to be like others, whose characteristics are charming in them alone. Being authentic, self-loving, without slipping into selfish ambitions, or pretending to be better than others is a victory over conflicts and complexes that torment and foster the depreciation of individuals embittered amidst inner struggles and outer failures.

When people accept themselves as they are, developing their inner resources in order to grow and acquire new moral qualities, they reach the summit of their aspirations without realizing it, and without suffering the perturbing impacts of the heights or the afflictions of the lower regions whence they have come.

Such behavior suggests the experience of love as enlightened selflessness devoid of the passions that belittle the sentiments. By loving, people strive to forget themselves in order to give of themselves. They feel enriched as they help others. This blooming of the affective sentiment is the glorious moment of self-realization – that instant in which individuals sing a hymn of enthusiasm to life, praising and glorifying it in themselves and their actions. This manifestation of love erupts from within like a soft and lovely rising sun, expanding as far as it can, but with one difference: it never sets, but continues to warm and illuminate.

As long as the sentiment of love in exchange for something persists – giving in order to get, or getting first and giving later – selfishness and a childish mindset remain in control, hampering real maturation.

The love that leads toward self-denial and away from perturbing passions, unreasonable demands and unjustifiable illusions is an inner accomplishment that dignifies and liberates.

In this developmental phase of the inner life, individuals begin to believe in their spiritual destiny, which is the enjoyment of happiness from then on, and since they are at peace regarding disruptive and depreciating factors, they advance without worrying about the turpitudes left behind.

Only by believing in their own potential and putting forth the effort to express it, despite the obstacles, can individuals successfully complete their *inner journey*, their self-discovery, and acquire the techniques that may be used to enjoy the benefits of such realization.

Upon reaching this stage, individuals feel the need to liberate themselves from things and fragile ties to past conditionings, which seemed to offer security – chimeras in a physical existence that can end at any moment. All belongings are worth the price assigned to them and should be considered to be of minor importance, despite their momentary usefulness. Freedom from one's belongings is a grand moment for psychological harmonization with life, whether in the body or outside of it.

When the implicit inner life is realized, it resurfaces in the realm of form in explicit manifestation. One is complete, free of impediments and rich in aspirations, without conflicts or complaints; hence fulfilled.

5

THE MEANING OF THE COMPLETE INDIVIDUAL

Foundations for Self-Realization.
Achievements that Fulfill. Life's Lessons.

FOUNDATIONS FOR SELF-REALIZATION

Jesus, the most remarkable psychotherapist humankind has ever known, said: *You are gods and you can do everything that I do and much more, if you so desire it.*[7] This is a proposition-challenge for psychologically mature individuals that are willing and prepared to go beyond the usual. To be successful, they must possess self-confidence and faith – that rational certainty between desire and the power to accomplish, leaving behind the perturbing "same old thing" of purely immediate, material ambitions.

Identifying oneself with a *god* means enhancing qualities that lie unknown and asleep within. A spark aware of its power of combustion produces a blaze when exposed to fuel. When people realize that they possess such a resource, they can light a fire that will consume their vices, thus freeing up virgin space for further personal development.

---

[7] A loose reference to John 10:34 and John 14:12 – Tr.

Those who are aware of their resources have the means to evaluate the potential for victory and they strive to achieve it, whereas those who are unaware give up under the pretext of their fragility, because deep down, they prefer it that way.

Psychological individuals have an important role, which must be detected and utilized with confidence. Their foundations rest on the deep layers of the unconscious – the experiences of the past – and on the enormous potential of the superconscious – the achievements they must succeed at – wrestling with the memories of yesterday and the ambitions of the future. These individuals oscillate between those two poles, which contribute to their happiness or unhappiness in the present, depending, of course, on their choices and efforts.

First, it is necessary to determine what the treasures actually are – both the internal and external ones – and then which ones take precedence and how to go about getting them.

Physiological individuals will prefer those of immediate significance and application, whereas *psychological individuals* will analyze those that take precedence and will acknowledge the external ones as being useful and the internal ones as being permanent. Without neglecting the former, they will devote themselves to acquiring the more valuable, permanent ones.

In this endeavor, they will identify with the realities that captivate them. They will discover that, on average, human beings experience 60,000 thoughts per day, which points to the grandeur and majesty of their mental organization, and they will realize how noble it is to learn to utilize such an abundant treasure, so often lost in a circle of mental corruption, wasting time and opportunity on lamentations, complaints, pessimism, and depletion of its strength.

They will recognize the need to be persons and not machines, avoiding monotonous repetitions that keep them from moving forward. They will apply ever more powerful, profound and useful thoughts to construct the best behavior for their peace-of-mind. They will eliminate perturbing thoughts, which can often be replaced, fostering a healthy mental climate that entails organic responses of well-being.

With this mindset, they will overcome the fear of getting sick, of aging, of becoming poor, of facing problems, of dying, for they know that all such factors are completely manageable, provided they assert their condition as *gods* and do all that is possible within the realm of personal effort.

Sickness is always a *bump in the road*; it is never a reality, but a temporary state that may be overcome even when it entails expiatory characteristics. Since the Self is eternal, organic or mental manifestations of this or that sort have to do with the transient nature of the world of form. Thus, the fear of sickness is unjustified.

Aging should not inspire any fear whatsoever. The beauty of each phase of the physical existence is to be found in the inner attitude of those observing the outer world. Experiences result from living, and making use of them requires time, during which the body ages and the spirit matures.

True poverty lies within, when aspirations involving inner growth and fulfillment are lost. Financial problems are always manageable if individuals will make an effort to overcome them, working to generate income while inwardly reassessing the meaning of life. Truly poor individuals are those who have lost their reason for living and have tragically handed themselves over to bad habits, mindless pleasures and the exhausting games of illusion…

...And death – that great *devourer* of life – is demystified and no longer inspires fear, for it is a part of the existential process, a way to develop the inner being, which experiences, step-by-step, new mechanisms for evolving.

The bearer of much beauty, the aging process is slow and biologically well-organized, providing a treasure trove of wisdom in the form of enlightened discernment. Aging is the propitiator of inner harmony and the ability to let go after the cycle of physical existence.

Learning to love everything one does, excelling at everything that one likes to do, sharing with everyone the joys and hopes of a triumphant life – all these give full meaning to the psychological individual, who can now *do everything* that Jesus did, identifying himself or herself with God.

Meanwhile, the *physiological individual* enjoys the benefits of the sensations, and remains entangled in the web of the passions until awakened by the jolts of the evolutionary process, jolts that may entail pain, profound worry, bitter disappointment – or the wonderful appeals of the love of beauty and the need for harmony and peace.

It is imperative to be awake to the reality of being, conscious of one's responsibilities and true objectives amid the existential challenges, discovering every meaning and thus evolving.

ACHIEVEMENTS THAT FULFILL

When childhood is filled with unsolved problems and challenges, these difficulties are transferred, by way of individuals' unconscious, to all the other phases of their lives. Psychological maturation becomes difficult, so they take permanent refuge in the infantile period, which continues to be problematic for them. At times, the need for self-punishment becomes overblown as a mechanism for justifying small acts of mischief, irresponsibility, lies or other reality-avoidance tactics, using means that are not always the best. Such cases may give rise to criminals, who, having been mistreated as children, feel the need to *punish* society for what happened.

To start with, they must rediscover their inner child and evaluate their level of growth, their needs and desires. If they still indulge in game playing, carelessness, shirking responsibility and blaming others, psychotherapy becomes urgent in order to help them grow and break free from the traumas of that phase.

It would not be fitting to remove the child aspect from the existential scenario; nevertheless, it should occupy its rightful place in the foundations of the unconscious so that it does not perturb the person as he or she now is. As a matter of fact, the presence of the child in all individuals is essential, for it renders life appealing and dream-like within the parameters of normalcy, which must always take precedence in every situation.

Good social ties are an important factor in individuals' fulfillment because, being *gregarious animals*, their coexistence with one another is a way for them to develop their aptitudes as they deal with the conflicts and confrontations that make up part of life, not slipping into animosity but developing tolerance and overcoming the arrogance of wanting to subject everyone else to their own standards.

Those who live alone avoid dealing with their own reality, which they see projected onto others. They fear living with others because they only know how to act in their own domain, where their will and desires rule, without sharing them or taking part in others' experiences.

Acquiring humility is part of the plan for inner growth. Individuals should avoid exhibitionism, as it tends to become perturbing due to the fact that it alters their vision of reality and themselves. They *offend* others with their presence by not being secure in their own values, which might actually offer harmony to their group. Humility starts with self-awareness, as individuals realize they are part of the universe, whose grandeur exposes their present *smallness* and just how much they still need to grow in order to grasp the majesty and harmony of the world in which they live. They do not become conceited by what they know, nor are they disheartened by how much they do not know. They are merely humble before life and they acknowledge the need to grow further and become better persons.

The unbridled struggle to possess more and more is common and it suffocates other aspirations, which yield to the predominance of the instinct of unrestrained possession. When the stage of psychological maturity is reached, the important thing is not to have more but to be more; that is, to increase one's inner qualities and moral/intellectual achievements without being ostentatious but aware of the victory over oneself and life's challenges, increasing one's endurance each and every day.

True happiness does not rely on what one has but on what one is.

A good example of this involved the case of a well-known TV ad personality, a woman who was hired due to her lovely looks, especially her smile. Her image impressed her viewers, who wanted to imitate her. They forgot that it was her job to smile and that she got paid for it; however, her usual mood did not match that reality.

Of course, one should smile because it is part of one's job, but the joy of living leads to smiling for the sheer pleasure and beauty of it. It is an invaluable self-therapy, for those who are comfortable with themselves are comfortable with the world.

On one of his customary trips to London, the famous Mahatma Gandhi opportunely took the time at the airport to observe the rich and pleasant-looking objects on display. As he carefully examined them, he beamed with pleasure. Concerned with such an unusual attitude in the man who had renounced all worldly things, a member of the English entourage said to him: *"If the Mahatma is interested in any of these pieces, it would be a great honor to offer them to him in the name of His Majesty."* The noble missionary, who had long-since found himself, smiled with neither disdain nor scorn and replied: *"No, I am very happy to just look at them and remind myself of all the things I no longer need."*

True health in its deepest expression is manifested as inner liberation, without the masochism of flights from the world, or assertions of one's own values by scorning and flogging one's body, as if it were responsible for one's weaknesses of character, imperfections of conduct, and psychological frustrations due to one's distorted vision of the world and its reality.

When true health does take root, individuals experience harmony in every situation. When with others, they feel the pleasure of coexistence, of being useful, and of giving and receiving attention regarding the manifestations of life. When alone, they fill up their time with enriching activities and thoughts; they do not feel lonely, despite being alone. Their mind is always their enquiring or compensating companion in relation to what they experience in terms of life's emotions.

It is obvious that all those who experience any kind of conflict will find it hard to feel psychologically compensated because their deficient inner structure will always reflect their struggles, and thus their ongoing anxiety and dissatisfaction.

Life's Lessons

The beauty of life lies in experiences that promote the development of the whole person. Born to succeed, the hurdles along the way are part of the process of reaching one's goals. Each successful step is a victory, a meaningful lesson that further increases one's patrimony. All thinking beings experience significant psychological opportunities as challenges of illumination and wisdom, although not all know how to use them properly. Wisdom unexpectedly blossoms even in the most perverse minds and coldest hearts; it opens up space for liberation from selfishness and for the acquisition of a sense of fraternity.

There are psychologically fertile moments that are highly suited for absorbing the lessons that life offers to each wayfarer of evolution. Not all manage to recognize this *magical time* in such a way as to profit from one's learning experience.

Louis XIV, called the *Sun King* in France, received a report that there was a plot against the throne. The informant was ordered to bring the king a list of suspects, who would be sentenced to death for crimes against His Majesty. However, when he was handed the list, the names of those who were conspiring against the monarchy were marked with a cross. This shook the king, for he saw the relationship. As a result, he declared: *"I cannot condemn them, because they are marked with the instrument with which the Innocent One was slain."* And he pardoned all of them.

The ruler's *conscience was asleep*. He was unconcerned about the future of the throne and his people, for he was in the habit of saying, "after me, the deluge." Consequently, he indulged in all sorts of pleasures and excesses. However, at that particular moment, he was touched in the recesses of his being by the symbol of shame with which they tried to silence the Great Voice, and he avoided becoming the impenitent executioner of an arbitrary condemnation that lacked due process of law, a condemnation in which the envoy's vile interests were obviously at play. Naturally, out of fear of going down in history – that great judge of the events of all times – as being unjust and his agents as being ignoble, he thought about the Innocent One and put a stop to the dreadful scheme.

Such is a life lesson for other lives, a lesson written in the pages of that turbulent existence and handed down to the future to guide other destinies. If only he had opened his mind to other attitudes of human dignity, rather than the personal and transitory interests that died along with his body.

Since individuals cannot escape from themselves – for they are always where their aspirations and needs may be found, despite psychological flights and mental excesses – the conscience expands and strengthens, tracing out the surest pathways with the accomplishments proposed by knowledge and lived by the sentiment.

In another instance, an ancient *koan* tells about a Chinese prince who was extremely proud of his collection of a dozen very old, rare porcelain plates marked by great artistic and decorative beauty. One day, in an unfortunate moment, their caretaker let one of them get broken. When the prince found out he was furious and condemned the

devoted servant – the victim of a fortuitous circumstance – to death. The news spread throughout the Empire, and on the day before the execution, a very old, wise man introduced himself and promised to restore balance to the collection. Taken with emotion, the prince gathered his court and accepted the offer. The venerable man asked for the remaining plates to be spread out on a skillfully embroidered, snow-white linen towel on a table. That done, the wise man approached the table, and to everyone's shock, he jerked the towel, brusquely casting the plates to the marble floor and shattering every one. Before the stupor that had come over the ruler and his court, he very serenely said: *"There you go, sir. All are the same, just as I promised. Now you can sentence me to death. Since those plates were worth more than people's lives, and considering the fact that I am old and have already lived longer than I should have, I sacrifice myself on behalf of those who would have died in the future when each one of the plates got broken. Thus, with my own life I mean to spare a dozen others, since, compared with the plates, they aren't worth anything."*

When the prince recovered from his shock, he was truly impressed. He freed his servant and the old man, grasping the fact that there is nothing more precious than life itself, especially human life.

Life offers the hardest lessons, inviting individuals to reflect.

Despite owning material possessions, when persons reach psychological maturity they place greater value on the possessions of the spirit, of a permanent reality, the loftier expressions of life.

The most precious possession is the existential opportunity, because it gives rise to all other occurrences and victories. It is individuals' inalienable patrimony on their evolutionary pathway. When they are lucid, they live their lives intensely each moment. They bloom on the spot where they find themselves and are not tormented by feeling they should be somewhere else. They lay down roots and evolve, free of the injunctions of unbridled ambition, perturbing passions and disquieting fixations. They are open to new accomplishments that further harmonize them. Consequently, they become an integral part of the universe, which invites them to master it.

In order to reach such a state and learn life's lessons, candidates must work inwardly and educate themselves, since by means of this priceless effort they change and grow spiritually, freeing themselves of pernicious atavisms and any leftover degenerative factors.

Education is an invaluable instrument for the constructing of happy individuals, who, in turn, become a living life's lesson for others following behind.

6

Aspects of Life

Youth and Old Age.
Being Awake. The Joy of Living.

Physical life is comprised of several aspects that make up one's existential reality. This reality, however, does not always imply real living: expressing oneself with conviction, taking full advantage of opportunities, and advancing joyfully without regretting the past or being anxious about the future.

A happy existence is not necessarily one that is short or long, but one that has been transformed into a message of joy and well-being for the individual, as well as for all those around him or her. Each life is a message, the contents of which ought to be positive in a way that contributes to other lives, enriching them with hope. Sickness and other problems are not aspects of unhappiness, but invitations by the physical body and life telling one it is necessary to be more lucid and aware. Along the same lines, death is not a failure of life but rather another, wonderful experience.

Psychologically mature individuals are capable of telling the difference between the authentic values connected with self-realization and the transitory values connected with material existence.

Thus, each phase of physical existence has characteristics that typify the developmental process of the structures of the personality and the individuality, enabling the storage of experiences that may be used to construct the ideal life, in which perturbing factors find no room to act to the detriment of healthy factors, which make up the whole of the self-realized individual.

The development of the individual is slow in every aspect, passing from one phase to the next without disquieting marks of incompleteness so that, in the next stage, one draws from the experiences of the previous stage, which will have been completed and consolidated on the foundations of the individuality.

All individuals reach maturity by means of different experiences. Some grow under the stimulus of ideals and aspirations cherished inwardly; others grow under the inspiration of beauty expressed in the arts, literature and culture in general; many are attracted to technology and the various resources of modern achievements; countless others are led by love and the need for fraternity, which they lovingly cultivate; the great majority, however, are *pushed* by suffering, the last choice for developing the inner resources that lie sleeping within.

Nevertheless, there are none who can stop the development of their higher being, even though it may be temporarily overwhelmed by those perilous enemies of the Self: limitation, ignorance, selfishness and its entire vile entourage.

Human beings pursue a grand destiny: complete self-realization under the attraction of Divine Thought, which permeates and dominates everything. Their transcendental origin leads them to return, inescapably, to their Higher Causality. However, as long as they remain unaware of that unyielding destiny, they move about in a circle of a limited emotional environment without Life's power of attraction having any influence on them whatsoever.

Thus considered, all the different aspects of Life are invaluable during one's physical existence and must be fully experienced.

YOUTH AND OLD AGE

People's hostility toward old age has become ontological, because, in their narrow, psychologically immature view of things, they equate it with decay, sorrow, loneliness, sickness and death. In their opinion, living entails cherishing permanently juvenile dreams, dehumanizing and fleeting sensations, going from one to the next amid dissatisfaction and inner turmoil.

Youth, in reality, is not just a biological state involving a particular age group. It is also the period in which individuals can love and feel, hope and live, and construct and experience new and edifying needs.

The juvenile period between infancy and the age of reason is highly significant for individuals' real development because it opens up space for learning, solidifying knowledge, and longing for accomplishments and achievement, all in a marvelous kaleidoscope. It is also a period of immaturity and wasted opportunities, because everything seems so distant and abundant that the loss of time and production has no real meaning. This gives rise to future conflicts that must be overcome.

However, youthful individuals are actually those who aspire to the ideals of human dignification, no matter what period of life they are going through. Holding on to the ability to fulfill and feel fulfilled, to produce and multiply, to renew and be renewed, they enjoy long-term, real youthfulness.

Old age sets in whenever individuals see themselves as useless, whenever they suffer the discredit of prejudicial society, which has developed concepts of life according to grossly materialistic, hedonistic standards.

Medical science continues to show that every period of life is rich with opportunities to learn, grow and develop the ability to solidify human values. The orthodox concepts of boundaries for the onset of old age – when signs of organic decay appear – have been completely surpassed.

Within this context, the mind is an important factor that generates incessant energies, in one sense or another, in a positive or destructive way, and as long as one can think with self-esteem and self-confidence, the limits imposed by age disappear, thereby facilitating the continuation of an enriching existence. By the same token, when young individuals let themselves become disheartened and start thinking destructively, they become imprisoned in the cellars of psychophysical decay and begin to wither.

The brain, which used to be little-appreciated regarding its incomparable capacity as the largest *gland* in the human body, is nowadays acknowledged as an extraordinary and unique harmonic network of seventy-five to one hundred billion neurons in a specialized and complex circuit, a most remarkable computer, which the mind has not yet been able to fathom. Its enzymes, cerebrin, globulins and other secretions control reactions throughout the body, laboring for physical and mental life. Nevertheless, the brain does not produce the mind. The mind originates in a causative source that precedes and succeeds the neuronal network. Weighing 1,300 grams, on average, it absorbs a remarkable amount of oxygen – 20% of the amount required by the entire body. Whenever a single nerve cell dies, the mind labors to keep the brain's components in order, widening and transforming its extremities into *trees (dendrites)*, which foster the flow of information without any break in continuity, producing marvelous electrochemical synapses, maintaining its own complete equilibrium and that of the body in general.

Still largely unknown and little utilized, the brain is a dynamic center of life, entailing the most complex operations imaginable. It is a transceiver antenna oriented to parapsychological bandwidths, yet it never loses its aptitude for receiving and recording within the bandwidth of normal consciousness.

Similar to muscles, which lose their tone and weaken if not exercised, the brain, if not excited by renewed mental energy, loses its ability to produce, because when nerve cells die, other cells do not branch out without new stimuli, and they fail to transmit the messages they are supposed to register, send and respond to.

For millennia, the brain remained almost completely neglected by science until it was studied and essentially *discovered* by Gall – physician, anatomist, and *father* of phrenology, just as Lamarck was the father of transformism. Until then, ideas about the brain were divided between philosophers, the *fathers* of medicine, and Patristic religion with its superstitions and ultramontane notions.

Passing through remarkable scholars, among whom were Cabanis and Broca, the probe of research penetrated the gray matter and deciphered its folds, which today give us a still very imperfect idea about its world of infinite information.

In the brain, therefore, lie the dispositions of youth and old age, depending especially on the mind, which vitalizes, activates and maintains it.

Still, many believe that old age means a loss of memory, deterioration of reasoning, emotional ups and downs... Of course, over the years the organic machinery does wear out and its capacity for production and effective results does decrease. Nevertheless, memory loss is not an exclusive symptom of aging, because many factors can contribute to it at any age: subtle infirmities such as urinary infections, medication poisoning, depression, Alzheimer's disease, etc. What matters is the individual's mental state, which determines the phase he or she is actually in and wants to remain in, whether it be extended youthfulness or premature old age.

The effort spent on one's mental state leads to wonderful results. It enables one to pursue one's duties, studies, searches and new accomplishments, without becoming exhausted or making excuses regarding the impossibility of growing and remaining young.

BEING AWAKE

Humankind, in general, lives in a sleep state, in lethargy, and that is why people suffer the worst sickness possible: ignorance of themselves, their destiny, and the meaning of their existence.

Comfortable with their situation, people may complain, but they do almost nothing to change society's ills, ills that are often characteristic of themselves as well; due to their masochistic need to inspire pity, they bemoan themselves. They yield to circumstances out of self-indulgence and make no real effort to overcome any obstacle that may pose a threat or hindrance to their progress.

Unconsciousness[8] prevails in the modern world because it gives in to immediate gratification, with no follow-up plan for attaining liberating emotions. Thus, society is divided into surreptitious, mutually hostile groups that grow further apart each day, whereas they should work together to eliminate separatist barriers and become aware of their infinite potential for self-realization and spiritual awakening.

But the moment inevitably arrives when individuals are induced to either awaken or remain dead to reality. In order to awaken from their heavy sleep, they must make every effort possible to break the chains of self-pity and unhappiness, self-deprecation and self-disrespect.

Being awake means self-fulfillment, being aware of one's inner reality and the infinite possibilities for growth that are within one's reach. It means freeing oneself from the

---

[8] Otherwise referred to as the *sleep-state consciousness* by the Spirit Author – Tr.

fears that keep one immobilized in uselessness, rediscovering the joy of living and acting, broadening one's communication with nature and all living beings, multiplying the means of human dignification and making them available to everybody; and submitting oneself to the eloquent purpose of enlightenment found everywhere...

The Apostle Paul was so convinced of the value of awakening to consciousness that, in Ephesians 5:14, he exclaims: *Wake up, you who sleep, rise from the dead and Christ will shine on you!* This is because sleep is a form of death, a wasted educational, enlightening, therapeutic, enriching opportunity. In this sense, when individuals are awake, Jesus illuminates them so that they may advance courageously in their search for self-identification.

All victors have been persons awakened to their endeavor and commitment to life, aware of their own worth without sentimentality and psychological flights of self-deprecation and self-punishment. Unfurling the banner of courage, they enter the battle, overcoming vices and developing virtues on the immense field of the conscience, like Krishna's proposal to Arjuna in the *Bhagavad Gita*, that marvelous canticle of psychological dignity and saga about a victor over his own passions...

Awakened individuals do not allow themselves the cunning of Sisyphus or the cruelty of Zeus, characters that felt the need to display their strength and power in the fragility of the immature and unconscious human being.

Thus, when Prince Siddhartha Gautama became the Buddha, that is, when he allowed himself to be enlightened by awakening from his lethargy, one of his disciples asked him after a lesson: *"Lord, have you found God? And if so, where?"* The missionary thought for a moment and then answered without preambles: *"After penetrating my own reality, I found God in my innermost being, in great serenity and dignifying activity."*

When individuals are awake, victories and discoveries are internal, resplendent and peaceful, powerful as lightning yet gentle as a morning breeze. Bearers of life, they lead other people to self-assurance, enabling them to understand those who remain asleep, who have no interest in self-awareness or the end purpose of existence. They do not become irritated, weary or upset with those who assail, persecute or seek to afflict them.

Upon meeting Jesus, Mary Magdalene awoke from her madness and was completely transformed. Paul of Tarsus woke up after Jesus called to him and he was never the same thereafter. Francis of Assisi accepted the Master's invitation and was reborn, abandoning the *old man* to become nature's cantor. After awakening to Reality, Leonardo da Vinci, Galileo, Newton, René Descartes, Pasteur, Albert Schweitzer and many others in the various fields of thought, science, art, religion and love, changed course and lifted humankind to a level of greater beauty and broader happiness.

Being awake means to evolve, free of prejudices and limitations, open to the good and to the truth, for which one has become a trailblazer and disseminator.

THE JOY OF LIVING

Life is a poem of beauty, whose verses are composed of luminous proposals written on the parchment of nature, which exalts its presence everywhere. Consequently, physical existence is a special opportunity for enchantment and accomplishment, by which the spirit beautifies itself and reaches the heights of Reality. There is sunlight and harmony everywhere, inviting us to peace and communion in its joyous ensemble. Only human beings, however, display sadness, marked by the moral briars they bear due to bygone attitudes and actions, badly kept promises and disastrous deeds, transferring from one stage to the next what they could resolve once and for all if they would only solve their problems from the inside out by means of well-directed efforts.

Thus, the joy of living should be an active part of intelligent individuals' personal transformation plan. They should enjoy all the magic on the canvas of the universe, taking from it the wonderful concessions of completeness that hover within the reach of all those who desire to grow spiritually, free of the torments and shackles of the past.

The destiny of human beings is freedom, for which they head with eyes set on the future. Being free means not being dependent, opting for what comprises their emulation for victory; having no anxiety about the past or the future, but living fully in the present in raptures of peace and joy.

As they mature psychologically, the joy of living is a powerful reason to pursue enlightenment. Such joy, of course, does not impede moments of pain-induced reflection, of yearning for love, of longing for health, of the presence of infirmity, of temporary anguish, or of anxiety about certain factors. Such phenomena, which make up part of the existential pathway, do not make joy impossible; instead, they give it a reason for being, because every challenge is followed by victory; every trial precedes achievement; every bout with suffering leads to a new level of balance, making joy a constant and a motivator for the production of new values.

Joy provides the brain with a larger amount of special, health-producing enzymes. Joy entails laughter, which is a powerful stimulant for the production of salivary immunoglobulin (sIgA), bearer of immunizing agents that provide constant organic balance by repelling the invasion of various viruses and harmful bacteria.

When people laugh, they stimulate key facial and general muscles, eliminating accumulated toxins that would poison them otherwise. Laughing is a means of expressing joy without shrill, nervous, uncontrolled cackling.

Nowadays, laughter therapy is an invaluable means to avoid certain contaminations and help with the healing of serious pathologies, especially crippling, infectious, degenerative diseases, and various emotional and mental disturbances.

The Gospel implies that Jesus rarely smiled. He was often seen weeping and almost never smiling: He, who presented Himself as *the most perfect being that God ever offered to humankind to serve as its model and Guide*, as the Spirits explained to the eminent Codifier, Allan Kardec. It seems paradoxical that He would weep... It is only an apparent contradiction. His tears were not due to suffering, but compassion, a superior and elevated sentiment of empathy toward individuals who preferred to remain in ignorance instead of taking advantage of His liberating lessons. It was a way for Him to show tenderness to the sick, who would have found in Him an effective therapy to deliver them from their embittering ills, which they considered of secondary importance, overpowered by the need to chase after what was pointless and ephemeral.

This is demonstrated when He speaks of His Good News of Joy and describes Himself as the *Door to the sheepfold, the Light of the world, the Way, the Truth and the Life, the Shepherd, the Messiah,* asserting that we are *the salt of the earth, the sheep, the needy* of every ilk, who need Him as Leader and Psychotherapist for the countless deficiencies and infirmities of the soul.

Self-knowledge reveals to individuals their potential and limitations, opening up room for renewal and the attainment of new horizons of health and plenitude, without a *guilty conscience*, without stigmas.

Consequently, psychoneuroimmunology has shown that good health can be attained by those who resolve to renew and believe in themselves, in their immense stores of energy, and in the value of their accomplishments. Completely compatible with the *Law of Cause and Effect*, positive accomplishments eliminate or diminish the weight of negative and harmful deeds.

Human beings are their psyche. According to how they act, thus will be the manifestations of the world of the I and the *Self.*

Well-constructed thought acts on the nervous system and brain, and together these produce protective enzymes that render the organism immune to the many invasions of destructive agents, thereby promoting health.

The joy of living is an invitation to a rich life filled with moral, spiritual, artistic, cultural, esthetic and noble productions.

Living well – one of the human goals – then becomes *good living*, a special, personal and non-transferrable accomplishment that can never be altered or lost, one that fosters happiness as people work for the peace that everyone craves.

7

DISCOVERING THE UNCONSCIOUS

Analysis of the Unconscious. The Process of Individuation. The Archetypes.

ANALYSIS OF THE UNCONSCIOUS

The eminent psychoanalyst Carl Gustav Jung established that the unconscious is a veritable ocean, in which the conscious is almost entirely immersed. The unconscious is like an iceberg, the visible part of which would be the area of the conscious – about 5% of the volume of that mostly uncharted mountain of ice. The conscious, according to Jung, may be compared to a *cork bobbing* in the enormous *ocean*.

In this way, one can get an idea of what the unconscious meant to the illustrious psychiatrist – his profession before he turned his sights to Psychoanalysis. In his profound research, he relentlessly tried to detect the presence of the unconscious, which would be responsible for nearly all the behaviors and programming of human existence, from the most primitive, automatic phenomena at its beginning, to the countless manifestations of a conscious nature.

One can find all the experiences of the individual stored up in that ocean, from his or her first expressions, across the periods of development and evolution, and up to the moment of the lucidity of *logical thought*, in which he or she now lives with the goal of attaining the highest level: *cosmic thought*.

It is very difficult for the unconscious to be disassociated from the different manifestations of human life, for it very powerfully dictates the events that comprise life's impulses and atavisms.

Nevertheless, one must bear in mind the presence of the spirit, which transcends effects and begins to exercise its function as the *unconscious*, the real reservoir of all the individual's experiences on the long, long anthropo-socio-psychological journey that he or she has inherited from successive reincarnations.

The *ego* participates in this entire process as the small part of the psyche that possesses *self-awareness* and self-identification. The ego is the "I" that recognizes itself as an individual with his or her own energies, which, in turn, are completely different from those of other individuals. The ego is the small part in us that perceives things and occurrences; it is the personality, as detected by the conscious.

The "I" invariably thinks only of itself, and does not comprehend the immensity of the unconscious, the totality of the self. This fact gives room to odd situations, such as when people refer to an incident they would never attribute to themselves. They insist that it was not them, that is, their conscious self, and they find it very surprising.

Every time the conscious mind realizes that the unconscious envelops it, it is shocked and amazed, since the unconscious is the totality, the *ocean* including the iceberg, which comes to the surface.

For Sigmund Freud, as well as for Carl Jung, the unconscious only expresses itself by means of symbols, and, using the delicate mechanisms of dreams and active imagination, these symbols can and should be sought out in order to be rightly interpreted so that their messages may be understood.

Dreams offer content that needs to be interpreted to facilitate the individual's development. By means of active imagination – bearing in mind that it is not fiction in the conventional sense, but a modality of creative thought – it is possible to enter the framework of the registers and reservoirs of the unconscious, opening its gates for a balanced release that will contribute greatly to the healthy conduct of the individual, enabling him or her to live a stable life.

We would like to take the liberty to add, however, that through concentration, prayer and meditation, as well as during some mediumistic trances, the unconscious can find additional means to facilitate the release of various feelings that lie within it, giving rise to the animic[9] phenomena so carefully studied by the esteemed Codifier of Spiritism – one of the identifiers of the archives of the unconscious, although under a different label.

Freud and Jung assert that formidable forces are at play in that extraordinary *ocean*, sometimes for and sometimes against the individual, who must decipher all of these mysteries in order to achieve both inner and outer

---

[9] Psychic phenomena produced by the incarnate spirit itself, without the intervention of other spirits (e.g. telepathy, telekinesis, psychometry, among others) - Tr.

self-realization. The unconscious contains the myths and fantasies, legends and superstitions of all peoples of the past and present, and in its deepest corners, parallel personalities are born or sleep, personalities that incorporate themselves into the individual's existence, generating conflicts and neurotic disorders.

However, according to both masters, the objective of interpreting such messages is not to immediately resolve neurotic disorders but to rightly utilize their forces, which bear energies for growth, elevation, knowledge and liberation.

The big challenge for human existence lies in the ability to explore that *unknown world*, and take from it all the potential that may produce happiness and self-realization.

Individuals usually go through life in an almost sleep-like state without any awareness of what is going on around them regarding events or their dynamics. They rarely take time to reflect, to ponder the objectives and needs of life per se. Everything happens to them automatically, fortuitously, affected as they are by the predominant physiological urges even during episodes of a psychological nature – and this is really regretful.

Consequently, they live unconsciously, far removed from reality, scattered, piling up conflicts and letting themselves be controlled by their dominant instincts.

Human existence is an invaluable learning experience that must not be wasted or lived utopically, as if it were a trip to fantasyland, where everything has its place in a timeless, mechanical way devoid of sense or reason.

The march of the evolutionary process is upward, and each day individuals must store up creative and enlightening experiences that will expand their field of development, leading them toward their cosmic destiny: complete freedom, plenitude. While in the body, they will suffer the positive or negative consequences of their acts, which are the building blocks of their future. That is why they must live consciously awake to the reality of living.

And that is also why focused thought is of inestimable value, in that it enables them to discover the archives that contain the past impressions that create difficulties or problems in their current behavior. At a deeper level, meditation is an invaluable instrument for their self-identification. It enables them to reach the more stratified structures of the personality to uncover archaic records that have become the creative foundations for their current conduct. Furthermore, prayer, besides assuaging their sentiments and soothing their afflictions, contributes to developing the phenomena of active imagination, liberating impressions which, by association, will broaden the field of their grasp of reality, exhuming and dispelling ghosts, and resuscitating traumas with the intention to heal them, thus clearing the field of perturbing images for the automatic mechanisms of dreams.

Despite all the invaluable contributions of psychoanalysis, we shall propose the conscious projection of the personality, that is, of the spirit on its *astral journeys*, through which, when lucid, it always experiences greater freedom and can thus overcome the effects of serious conflicts from past incarnations stored up in the unconscious.

This *conscious immersion* in the structures of the complete Self facilitates the release of conflicting images from the spirit's past and recent present, giving rise to the harmony needed for the preservation of health, now enriched with superior accomplishments.

So long as individuals do not discover the *reality* of their unconscious, they may continue to suffer from neurotic disorders – the result of fragmentation, existential emptiness, the lack of psychological meaning – because they identify only a tiny part of what they call reality. They feel isolated, without proper guidance for solving the various problems that afflict them, and consequently they escape to seek fulfillment in neurotic states.

This *emotional downfall* causes them to lose their sense of religiosity, for, according to Freud and Jung, the unconscious is where one finds the presence and meaning of God, the spirit, and perceptions regarding the Divinity... To Freud and Jung, when individuals remain ignorant of the potential of the unconscious, they break the connections with their deep Self, and therefore the mechanisms that would lead them to an understanding of God, the soul and eternal life.

It is in the unconscious that we find the presence of the spirit in the folds of the inner being, impregnated with memories that do not reach the current conscious, and yet affect behavior indirectly, causing disquieting and unfamiliar states within the structure of the ego. Self-identification, i.e. self-discovery, enables individuals to grasp the need for progress while at the same time it disarticulates the difficulties that have been formed by negative past life experiences, the *vestiges* of which continue to cause problems.

Only upon beginning to experience and understand one's inner reality, engaging in self-discovery and remaining awake to the activity of *logical* and conscious *thought,* are the damaging effects of the past released and new guidelines for future conduct set forth. It is then that freedom for creative activity is acquired, without the shackles of *guilt*, which always sets in after any questionable attitude or harmful action.

Individuals are manifestations of the Divine Thought, which created them for dynamic self-realization.

Consequently, they must stop ignoring their *inner world*, their *unconscious*, and dive into the depths of themselves, embracing self-discovery without traumas or shocks, anxieties or disturbances, in a process known as **individuation**.

All this energy, borne by the unconscious, can be harnessed for self-edification, the overcoming of fears and perturbations, the daily ghosts responsible for the individual's insecurity and emotional instability.

With remarkable astuteness, Jung stated that individuals bear many symbols that sleep in their unconscious in a great plurality, which must be worked on until a sense of unity is reached, a unification of opposing terms in a single expression of equilibrium. Thus, Jung used the expressions *yin* and *yang* – present in everyone's lives – to represent the masculine (yang) and the feminine (yin). The former is active, dynamic, strong and rich in movement, heat and clarity. The latter is passive, restful, fragile, without much activity; it is cold, shadowy[10] ... These apparent opposites produce conflicts, because the moment one thinks about doing something, an opposing idea immediately surfaces; one wants to proceed and hold back at the same time; a challenge arises to try to achieve something, while another

---

[10] Here, the terms "masculine" and "feminine" are not gender attributes, but symbolic illustrations of psychological characteristics. – Tr.

part strives to counter new experiences. These are, most assuredly, masculine and feminine dynamics that lie latent within the individual.

In antiquity, eastern mysticism, in the form of wisdom, endeavored to stimulate individuals to handle each of these two forces in a balanced way, allowing one or the other to be predominant, depending on the situation, ultimately producing balance, which is the result of the harmony of control – at the proper time – by this or that inner dynamic.

In this harmonious phase, it is possible to tell the difference between what is good and what is bad, what is just and what is arbitrary, identifying the opposites, thus giving oneself a sense of perfect balance, of oneness with the cosmos. Is this not the attainment of *cosmic thought*, when the Divine Consciousness unfolds within the human being and he or she can exclaim as Jesus Christ did: **"The Father and I are One"**?

Jung went on to identify a duality in human beings, ever-present in dreams, to which he gave the labels *animus* and *anima*. The *animus* is the masculine representation in women's dream activity, and the *anima*, the feminine representation in that of men. These two dynamics repeat the great mythological, historical, religious figures in stories, fairytales and myths of peoples of every epoch, and they provide psychological associations and experiences, according to each person's inner structure.

Agreeing completely with the thought of the remarkable researcher of the human psyche, we would only dare propose that, in such dream-related representations, many of the *animus* and *anima* characters are the reminiscences, the revivals, of past lives stored in the unconscious, thanks to the perispirit or *intermediary body* between the spirit and the material body.

Jesus, for example, harmonized the two *natures*: the *animus*, when it was necessary to use powerful energy and will to upbraid hypocrites and press on fearlessly on behalf of the ideal of love, and the *anima*, whenever He attended to the unfortunates who sought Him out, in need of understanding and aid. No one like Him has ever achieved such perfect harmony between the *yang* and *yin*, proving Himself to be *the most highly evolved spirit that God has ever offered to humankind to serve as its model and guide*, according to the response of the Messengers-to-Humanity to Allan Kardec in *The Spirits' Book*, question no. 625.

Love takes precedence in that profound endeavor of self-identification, and it must be molded consciously in order to develop. It is inherent in human nature, originating from all of Nature, which is the Work of the Love of God, who filled it with that *sentiment*, structuring it in the harmonious vibration that prevails even when opposing forces collide.

This *archetype* of Jungian thought – love – makes up part of the immense listing prepared to translate the images imbedded in the human unconscious, but which many psychoanalysts advocate could be expanded, depending on each person's aptitude – taking into account his or her own dream experiences – growing increasingly broader to encompass every possibility and avoiding constriction.

From the unconscious, to the conscious, to **individuation**, the individual can become harmonized, achieving peace and total health.

Joanna de Ângelis / Divaldo Franco

THE PROCESS OF INDIVIDUATION

The multifaceted experiences of reincarnation leave an infinite repository of characteristics in the individual's innermost being. We may identify these characteristics as being the Jungian *archetypes*, ancestral inheritances transformed into a voluminous amount of material, dictating the unfolding of events that drive individuals to display different behaviors in their daily lives.

All individuals are the sum total of their past lives, in which diverse personalities have constructed their mental reality, with a whole load of conflicts and struggles that have left deep marks on them.

Being able to dive into that tumultuous ocean of past experiences is the purpose for coming into awareness.

In order to achieve success, each individual must see him or herself as unique and different, despite having all the similarities that are common to all the other members of the immense human family.

Normally, individuals take as standards those who seem to be better, authentic role models, and they seek to emulate them. They forget the fact that it is impossible to achieve positive results in such an attempt, because, as they imitate others, they lose their own identity and character. They mold themselves to false formulas and idols that also struggle and disguise their own needs in the exteriorization of their personality.

The grand psychological endeavor of individuals' growth resides in their search for themselves. Although similar to other people – in terms of the physical matter of which all are made – each person is different.

Psychologically, everyone's unconscious contains all the symbols of all the different cultures mixed together to form the individual *reality*. However, it is indispensable for them to seek **individuation**, that is, authenticity, ideally constructing and accepting themselves with qualities that are non-transferrable and peculiar to them alone. In this process, they must work on their own moral transformation, uncovering everything that is troubling them and striving to overcome it by elimination, without generating trauma or dissatisfaction, thus dissipating the condensations of past lives, through their becoming aware of their inner completeness, which is now in harmony with their outer manifestations.

This process may take an entire lifetime, something which is very healthy because individuals can find that they are undergoing continual renewal for the better, freeing themselves from the negative burdens that used to dictate their reactions and cause them problems in the form of inner disturbances that affect their behavior.

Becoming a complete, original and unique individual is the goal of **individuation**. Individuation frees the conscious from the strongest constrictions of the dominating unconscious. Consequently, it is indispensable to confront the unconscious serenely, exposing it and integrating it to the current conscious by the best means possible. Individuals find their own pathway, which they must follow confidently, working continuously, without guilt, anxiety, unjustifiable fears, or conflicts responsible for regrets…

Despite being members of a specific social group, individuals must find their own interests, maintaining, at the same time, the values and qualities that are inherent to the group as a whole, so as to not alienate themselves from the context in which they relate and live.

Despite their similarities, individuals have their own psychological structure that necessarily results from experiences lived in different physical existences. Only reincarnation can explain that multiplicity of people's psychological content, making them distinct from one another. Although they all proceed from the same *trunk*, each one has lived in very unique and different situations.

In seeking **individuation**, it is to be noted that the contributions of the outer world impress on certain individuals values that are not authentic for their level of maturity and that the only genuine values are those that proceed from their inner being, their unconscious, which is now in attunement with the lucid conscience. This provides much peace-of-mind because it enables individuals to understand that, in order to succeed, they do not have to be like everyone else, a copy of models portrayed in the media, in successive celebrations of self-delusion and widespread torment.

All individuals possess unlimited wealth in their inner world, which is their divine inheritance, and which now awakens and renders them conscious, freeing them from perturbing atavisms.

The human psyche, which has been constructed as a result of existent universal symbols, expands during individuation. Individuation waits to be attained by all thinking beings and, on the other hand, it is also the goal of reincarnation: the attainment of the Self, the elevation of the spirit hovering over the ruins of bad experiences that have been transformed into edifices of peace.

THE ARCHETYPES

The concept of the *archetype*, adopted by Jung, was already known by Philo Judaeus in his references to the *Imago Dei*, the divine image that exists in the human being. According to Jung, it can also be found in Irenaeus, who stated in turn: *"The creator of the world did not fashion these things directly from himself, but copied them from archetypes outside himself."*

Actually, the *archetype* comes from the Platonic notion regarding the primordial and terminal *world of ideas*, from which everything begins and to which everything returns.

Jung employed Platonic thought to refer to the universal images that have been preexistent in the individual – or which proceed from the first individual – from time immemorial.

These symbols remain in people's unconscious, regardless of any other psychological constructions, making them similar to one another and giving them *uniformity of experience*, becoming a representation that persists imaginatively. Such images have been common to all peoples and characteristics of the human species ever since its beginnings. They arise spontaneously and have various configurations in the myths and symbols of all cultures.

The word *archetype* comes from the Greek *arkhe*, which means *first*, and *typon*, which means *mark, stamp, model*; thus, it means the first, initial marks or models that make up the psychological framework of the individual, providing the identification of the human creature. The archetypes exist in the individual as an inheritance, as an integral part of his or her process of evolution.

Quite often these *archetypes* appear in dreams as preexistent images that have broken free of the unconscious. However, not all symbols derive from the *archetypes*, because they may originate in the individual's own energy, in his or her current fixations, psychological traumas, conflicts, frustrations, anxieties and desires. The *archetypes* differ from such inherent energy, in that the archetypes have a universal character, whereas the others are unique to the individual.

In considering the universality of the *archetypes*, there is a large variety of symbols, which were classified by Jung and afterward by his adherents and successors. However, they cannot have a set number, because they always present themselves with individual characteristics in natural variations, deriving from the patterns and signs of each personality.

Jung stated that the term *soul*, adopted by religions, appeared naturally due to the *archetype*, which has its psychological counterpart. Thus, in the woman, the soul would be masculine and have an inner existence, which is *married to Christ*, in the concept of the Pauline union and the woman's *spiritual marriage* to Jesus, whereas in the man it is feminine, as being his inspiring muse, responsible for poetic, literary and artistic beauty in general. This psychological representation appears as the *anima* in men's dreams and as the *animus* in women's dreams.

If a person has dreamed about the *devil*, it does not necessarily mean that he or she actually had contact with him, but rather with the *archetype* symbolic of the evil that has existed in the unconscious of all peoples from the beginning, and which has remained down through the millennia. Likewise, angels, love, hate, etc., are symbols that have always existed within individuals, and have been handed down through the collective unconscious, exerting a preponderant role in dream language and existential behavior.

These symbols emerge and hold sway in people's psychological lives without their being aware of it, appearing even in the banal events common to daily life.

Whenever people refer to other persons, extolling their stoicism or citing their cowardice, they are identifying the archetype that lives in their own unconscious, and which has a general character that is common to all. Hence, people always see in others the archetype that is inherent to themselves, a fact that helps recognize it.

Individuals are multidimensional, possessing common characteristics that derive from the perfect grouping of the *archetypes* that comprise each individuality. This enables people to understand others and identify with their values, qualities and sentiments.

The *archetypes* usually appear shrouded in mystical, divine symbols, with characteristics of reality, or in the form of fantasies, which dreams unveil in a decisive manner.

Although we agree in part with the eminent master, we will add that many symbols that present themselves as archetypes actually derive from another type of primordial inheritance: each spirit's experience resulting from the vast ocean of its reincarnations. Thanks to reincarnation, past lives are transmitted from one stage to the next, with those that were the most influential prevailing as determinants of current behavior, thereby establishing, in the individual and deep unconscious, symbols that appear in dreams or in the waking state as various conflicts in need of release.

Reincarnation explains the presence of the *archetypes* in human beings because they are heirs to their own accomplishments down through time, acquiring, at each step of the way, values and knowledge that remain stored in the folds of the eternal being that they are.

While the illustrious master located all gods and geniuses, heroes and models of the Greek Pantheon, including those of other cultures, as being the presence of symbols that generate the *archetypes*, the study of reincarnation has demonstrated that, even in the form of symbols, some of the legends and myths in the history of cultures result from spiritual inspiration, from insights experienced by countless persons, hence also confirming the fact that the spirit preexists the body and survives it after death.

These *primordial types*, taken from the trappings of legends, which belong to the development of thought in its various levels of growth until it reaches the *rational*, the *logical*, have always existed, not only in the imagination, but in reality, which fantasy adorned and perpetuated as mythological figures.

Of course, as Jung stated, these archetypes appear in dreams as divine, religious personalities, bearers of transcendental content and presented as supernatural, invincible. In many circumstances, however, they are encounters with transpersonal beings that have survived death, and which inhabit not only *the world of ideas* – in the Platonic conception – but that of energy that predates the material, the organic, and which is causal and extemporal.

Thus, in a transpersonal view of events, we can associate the *archetypes* to another type of lived, inborn reality embedded in the deep unconscious – the spirit itself – dictating current behaviors, entailing spirit-related, parapsychological and mediumistic experiences.

Delving into the ocean of the unconscious, seeking to eliminate conflicts dating back to various past events – from the current and previous incarnations – in order to reach **individuation**: such is the goal for those who desire to awaken and be aware of their reality, struggling for inner enlightenment and complete happiness.

8

URGENT: SELF-AWAKENING

The Awakening of the Self.
The Endeavor to Achieve Balance. Discipline
of the Will. Liberating Actions.

THE AWAKENING OF THE SELF

The initial phase of life, considered from whatever aspect, is one of sleep. For that very reason, the psyche "*sleeps* in the mineral, *dreams* in the plant, *feels* in the animal, and *thinks* in the human being," as synthesized very appropriately by the eminent Spiritist philosopher Leon Denis. And it continues, with immense intuitive capacity, in the *pure spirit,* continuously acquiring new experiences forever.

Individuals are destined for perfect attunement to Cosmic Consciousness, which sleeps within, awaiting factors that foster their development, that is, their ongoing awakening.

Awakening, therefore, is indispensable. They must abandon the lethargy that proceeds from the stages through which they have passed and break free of their apathy – manifested as unconsciousness – to pursue transcendent realities, ridding themselves of the progress-hindering restrictions that enslave the Self to left-over, sleeping passions lying in the deep unconscious, which continues to send out pessimistic, troubling messages.

Becoming aware of who one is and what one must do in order to be successful constitutes an urgent calling, and is an invaluable contribution to undertaking the urgent task of a transforming inner revolution.

Quite often, we discover in human behavior references to *sleeping, being asleep, asleep*, characterizing people's existential states. Most people certainly are *asleep* to their own realities, to the challenges of evolution, to the attainments of the Self. They are infatuated with immediate petty interests, enshrouded in darkness, or enthralled by unhealthy narcissism, and they would rather remain in a state of *sleep consciousness* than experience awakening to lucidity, and therefore, to commitments regarding life and to inner growth, which is like a veritable childbirth. Awakening to a new reality about life is like undergoing a profound, liberating, *painful yet happy*, inner childbirth.

In other cases, some people, who do want to awaken, seek out famous *gurus* of their time to have them think and act in their stead, without the personal effort of those who actually become their disciples (*chelas*). This stimulates the paralysis of their limbs and body in lengthy, unproductive states of prolonged meditation, inappropriately avoiding the constructive endeavors of real life, which is always challenging and demanding. Such behavior is a form of transference of responsibility that is far removed from a serious commitment to self-effort, which is the sole means for individuals to find their reality and shape it, broadening their capacity for development.

Fortunately, the moment comes when true *masters* and *guides* do show the way, but they require their students to advance by themselves, overcoming the distances – especially the inner ones – that separate them from the eternal Self.

Psychology, in turn, invites individuals to advance without using new types of *crutches* or other forms of dependency in order to be free. It is understandable that, at the beginning of their learning experience, candidates are supported by their instructors, from whom they gradually break free to win their own space.

Revolutions regarding thought have been very fast, especially in this decade, which foretells a New Era of Consciousness when horizons will be broadened and people's understanding will be fuller, especially regarding the Self, the immortal spirit.

With a few exceptions, all the currents of present-day philosophy, and the experiments conducted by psychological and parapsychological approaches (as well as by other approaches) focus on the permanent, real being, that which crosses the portal of death and then returns to the earthly scene in a new, illuminative experience.

Consequently, the search for Reality has been oriented toward the inner world, into which the individual plunges with enthusiasm and wisdom, overcoming the imperatives of the perturbing passions and most-primitive sensations.

This proposal is very old because people's needs are also very old. One can cite the Gospel of Jesus. The Gospel is a veritable treatise on psychotherapy and everyone should reread it from a deep, new perspective, especially according to what is happening in psychology and other approaches to the psyche. In the Gospel, individuals are referred to as *being asleep, sleeping* and also as *awakening*.

When Jesus went to visit the apparently dead Lazarus, he approached the tomb and said that his friend was *sleeping*. He ordered the stone to be rolled away and commanded Lazarus to awaken and come out of the darkness. When the cataleptic heard that voice resound in the acoustics of his soul, he awakened, regained consciousness and came out of the tomb without the need for any kind of miracle. Jesus perceived that death had not actually seized Lazarus' spirit, and that it had not yet broken the powerful ties of the *perispirit*; therefore, Lazarus was still alive, although *asleep*.

It was an organic sleep brought on by catalepsy, because Lazarus had already *awakened* to Reality, which was why he could hear the call to return.[11]

Following in Jesus' footsteps, the Apostle Paul repeated this act of awakening many times in different situations, depending on the degree of sleep state of his listeners or those interested in his message.

In his letter to the Romans, after a few other considerations, the trailblazer to the Gentiles wrote: *I say this because you know the time has come for you to awaken from the sleep…*[12] that keeps people distracted and removed from the Truth in permanent indecision, endless demands, pointless arguments or fruitless, superficial searches – all these being escape mechanisms to avoid pursuing liberating knowledge.

The sleep state is a paralysis of the soul, a weight on the individual's conscience and a detriment to the community's; thus it is pleasing for all who consciously or unconsciously

---

[11] John 11:11 – Spirit Auth.

[12] Rom. 13:11 – Spirit Auth.

avoid the highly serious responsibilities regarding the Self as well as for society, which they exploit and upset with their dependence.

Still examining the issue of sleep, the *Liberator of the Gentiles* urged in his letter to the Ephesians: *Wake up, you who sleep, and rise from the **dead***.[13]

This appeal is obviously addressed to those who, although alive physically, are dead to the reality of the Self. They are in hibernation regarding the wonderful qualities of their immortality.

Those *dead* to the higher emotions pass through the world sodden with the passions, to which they are anchored in a dreadful state of intoxication, suffering their martyrizing injunctions. They are *living corpses*, according to a Gospel allegory. Whenever they are invited to aim higher, to ennobling ideals, to stronger ethical values, they make excuses and refuse to cooperate. They say that life has other purposes and they pamper themselves with food and other pleasures, which soon pass, leaving them empty and starved. Their awakening is always painful because it is very hard for them to abandon their unhealthy habits and adopt new ones, which, at first, seem strange, incomplete, and senseless.

When they are awake and clear about the essential objectives of life, individuals get up and leave the crowd of others who are still **dead** to reality.

Pursuing the same therapy, the renewed Apostle Peter grasped what had happened to him; thus he warned his followers: *While I am still in this tabernacle, I think it right to awaken you with a reminder…*[14]

---

[13] Eph. 5:14 – Spirit Auth.

[14] 2 Pet. 1:13 – Spirit Auth.

It is worthwhile to see the body as a *tabernacle*, in which the purification of the senses is possible, rendering it necessary to *awaken* others by means of *reminders* of all that has happened and been forgotten; of all the events of life that now lie in oblivion; of all the values that used to signify hope and dignity, but which are now abandoned. By means of this returning to live – the *reminder* – a healthy awakening and peaceful life are possible.

Impartially examining these proposals of awakening, one can see that the matter is urgent, despite the time that has elapsed since the warnings contained in all the doctrines of human dignity.

One should pay special attention to the experience of Peter in the moments before his denial of his Friend and the unforgettable tragedy of Calvary, after having been lovingly warned: ...*This night, before the cock crows, you shall deny me three times...*[15] foretelling his defection due to still being asleep to the high calling of acting in line with his Benefactor when called to bear witness – which is always a test of psychological and existential maturity.

It seemed that Jesus' prognostication could not possibly materialize; yet it did, and with the richness of detail with which it was foretold, calling Peter to a true awakening, which made him give of himself up until the last moment...

As one continues revisiting the Gospel of Jesus, one will notice that His discourse is always filled with warnings to those who are asleep, whether physically, morally or intellectually.

Another time, for example, while Jesus was communing with God just before His humiliation, He stopped three

---

[15] Matt. 26:34 – Spirit Auth.

times to check on His companions. They were supposed to be keeping watch, but were asleep, anesthetized either by indifference or by their inconsequential state of consciousness. After repeated attempts to wake them up, He finally let them be, since it was already too late and would do no good.

The challenge of sleep is great due to the lengthy period of permanence in the early stages of evolution that individuals pass through during their spiritual growth.

The unconscious is in control of the sensations and emotions, leaving little room for consciousness, for acting lucidly. Nevertheless, when Jesus told Peter about his denial and the crow of the rooster, one could infer that the unconscious was represented by the symbol of the noisy rooster that wakes individuals up, something which, in Peter's case, would only happen once remorse assailed his sleeping awareness.

Awakening is urgent because it liberates and confers authority on one's discernment. The ability to understand is such that an optimistic and clear vision becomes the foundation of one's psychological behavior, and thus of the internal mechanism for acquiring happiness.

This does not happen only when everything is going well, but also in the face of circumstances normally regarded as unfortunate. Then, instead of being rebellious or desperate, amid the serenity of being awake, one can ask oneself: *What is this perturbing event trying to tell me?* If it is sickness, a physical, emotional or mental problem, a monetary loss or the loss of employment – one's means of making a living – one can ask oneself: *What does this mean for my progress? What are the reasons behind these messages?*

As one journeys within – harmoniously and with a sincere desire for self-discovery – and seeks to find the destabilizing factor, the conscience identifies the real cause and works on it, managing the profound dystonia that manifests in a troubling manner.

Such behavior provides security, focus on the ideal, harmony, and balance.

When asleep, individuals move from one dependency to the next, seeking guides and leaders to think for them and assume responsibility on their behalf.

When one goes deep within the Self, coherence arises regarding life and its possibilities; one works on being released from all enslaving ties. One does not look for pre-fabricated models or univocal forms that work for everybody. Each person has his or her own characteristics and resources. This does not stimulate perverse individualism, but rather the acquisition of one's own identity. Nevertheless, there is one Guide and Model, whose exemplary life has endured all the storms of time and all the acerbic and pungent criticisms of many thinkers: Jesus, the true *divider of the waters* of history.

Psychologically whole and awake, He was the greatest example of full Consciousness ever known in the evolution of the individual, teaching without presumption, loving without caprice, and sacrificing Himself without any masochistic leanings.

The bearer of health par excellence, He never displayed any kind of disturbance such as excitement or depression, even during the hardest times on a pathway marked by the incomprehension of His contemporaries.

Simple and unadorned, His behavior was optimistic, rich with beauty and tenderness, demonstrating unequivocally His moral and intellectual ascendancy.

Always awake, Jesus is the maximum exponent of the attainment of the Self.

THE ENDEAVOR TO ACHIEVE BALANCE

In every process of psychological maturation – awakening to consciousness – there is a game of interests that may be synthesized as the real-life experiences that have shaped the individual's personality, creating habits and behaviors, and the aspiration to what one hopes to accomplish, confronting struggles and endless challenges until the habits of a new reality are forged.

This is an all-out struggle due to crystalized impulses in the *already done* and one's uncertainty regarding future aspirations.

In this endeavor, one may fail by falling into one excess or another, by abandoning a new experience and becoming complacent, or by relentlessly and irrationally striving to reach a goal that lies beyond one's current possibilities. In any situation, the ideal is always balance, which is a way to measure one's achievements.

Balance entails harmony between what one aspires to, what one accomplishes, and how one behaves emotionally, without being anxious about what one should produce or being conflicted about what one has achieved. It is an inner achievement capable of measuring, without a static paradigm, the worth of one's achievements. By detecting failures in one's past behavior, one can peacefully rebuild one's pathway and correct one's mistakes, and whenever success is achieved, one should expand it serenely, without extravagance or presumptuousness, understanding that one is only at the threshold of inner development, of the profound maturation of the psychological being.

Balance results from identifying the various resources that lie dormant in the deep unconscious, which, once tapped, open the way for the awareness of one's duties and responsibilities. Only by means of a constant effort at self-identification is it possible to achieve the harmony needed to act, initiating one's conduct in the mental arena by means of cultivated thoughts, which become stimuli for the struggle.

Protagoras of Abdera stated: *"Man is the measure of all things."* Reality is an ongoing process of becoming, where the truth varies according to the times and according to the evolutionary stage of the human being. However, Heraclitus stated: *"Nature loves to hide"* in a challenging proposal so that the reason for all things may be found, for the inattentive eye only sees the edges and never nature per se. For Heraclitus, seeing is an integral part of saying and hearing, in a triad comprising "man's" reality.

In a more profound analysis, nature is hidden, for it sleeps in the collective unconscious of all observers, in their atavistic inheritances, in the various achievements of times and peoples, each observer *discovering* a part of the whole until reaching the *threshold of seeing, the capacity of saying, and the faculty of hearing* beyond the physical senses.

On the other hand, that "man," whom Protagoras stated to be *the measure of all thing*s, is reminiscent of the natural process of evolution in the different periods – anthropological, sociological, psychological – advancing toward awareness and full self-identity.

The Self acquires experiences by means of successive reincarnations, overcoming conditionings and dependencies by enlightening the conscience, which imposes balance for attaining emotional well-being and integral health.

The Laws of Balance are everywhere, maintaining cosmic harmony. At the same time, they are inherent in the microcosm, establishing and preserving the rhythm of molecular agglutination. In the moral realm, balance is the ability to gauge the values that are appropriate for inner peace and the need to continue to evolve without the shocks that result from changes in frequency fields and behaviors, which every new state produces.

The effort to become balanced is the effective means for self-realization and for remaining awake. It is well-directed, purposeful action, by which the will may be disciplined to reach its enlightened goal.

Work is the appropriate means for this endeavor, in addition, of course, to the inner journey. Outer work is accomplished in *horizontal time*, in conventional hours devoted to the acquisition of resources for maintaining bodily existence, in which the achievements of the intelligence, reason, strength, and physical resiliency are invested. Inner work, on the other hand, takes place in *vertical time*, which is unlimited due to its intrinsic nature.

Work of any kind is love in action, when ennobled by the sentiments. *Horizontal* work sustains the body; *vertical* work sustains life. Work may be done in the spirit of beneficence, without customary payment or even expectations of gratitude or kindness; selflessly, as one discovers oneself and develops the real qualities of the spirit, understanding that serving is an existential goal, and that loving spells deliverance from the ever-changing ego.

Balance attained while serving is a mark of progress, a living lesson of awakening, and one does not become exhausted or discouraged if one's desired purposes are not achieved as planned.

Merely striving for balance already sets a new course for one's life, overcoming perturbing, *egotistical* conditionings reminiscent of the immediate instincts of eating, sleeping and procreating... Physical existence is more than automatisms; it is a passionate process of becoming, which is accomplished step-by-step, culminating in self-awareness.

Effort, in this psychological context, may be described as the tenacity not to let oneself be overcome by stagnation or conformity, or be limited by what has already been achieved. It is an investment of the will to grow further, to reach new levels, ridding oneself of every obstacle that holds the spirit back.

DISCIPLINE OF THE WILL

The *faculty of representing an act that may or may not be carried out* – as defined by the good lexicographers – the will must be directed by means of mental discipline strengthened with meditation and lofty thoughts in order to create new conditionings, thereby forging different habits.

There are three indispensable resources that support the will's framework: patience, perseverance and self-confidence.

Patience teaches that while every endeavor has a beginning, it cannot be finished right away, for just as soon as one phase is completed, another challenging one appears, since the individual never stops growing. Only through careful and continuous action can one reach one's objective.

Thus work unfolds peacefully, as new horizons open up to be braved at a later time; one never feels rushed or troubled for not yet having completed it.

Patience is a resource that must be trained insistently to give continuity to any undertaking while one waits for outside factors to contribute to the hoped-for results.

This mechanism is nothing but the result of well-directed effort, a rhythm in one's work that must not be interrupted.

Conditionings are slowly created in the unconscious to aid the ability to wait, quieting perturbing anxieties and fostering a climate of emotional balance.

Like any other achievement, patience requires the indispensable requisites of practice, consistency, and faith in one's ability to carry out the endeavor. Patience avoids going beyond what is required for one's inner growth at the start, preparing a plan that must be followed step-by-step, without leaps, bringing excellent results that will open the way to other possibilities for personal development.

In the tradition of early Christianity, people regarded as saints those individuals endowed with uncommon attitudes, capable of handling unbearable situations and even excruciating testimonies. Over time, various legends arose, much to the taste of the imagination. For instance, it was said that St. Kevin, desiring to pray, was seized by an attitude of ardor and held out his arms through an open window in preparation. Suddenly, a warbler landed on one of his up-turned palms, where it proceeded to build a nest.

Two or more weeks passed but Kevin did not move until the little bird had hatched its eggs.

His companions regarded this as an act of patience – blessed and unusual patience!

It is not necessary to reach that degree of patience. It is obviously impossible to live it; even so, the example serves to show that, with patience, the impossible becomes possible.

Next is perseverance as an indispensable factor for disciplining the will.

Perseverance entails tenacity and persistence in the endeavor one is undertaking or plans to undertake, such that the course is not interrupted. Even when challenges manifest, firmness of decision on what one will carry out instills more interest in the process, helping one to finish the project without discouragement taking hold and working against it.

Only with perseverance can one shape one's ambitions to one's acts, making them accomplishable, materializing them, especially those of lofty moral character, the ones that result in blessings for the spirit.

When not disciplined, people abandon the effort needed to reach their goals. They believe they do not have the moral character to continue; yet, when they find themselves in a pleasurable and pleasing situation that caters to their unhealthy side, they let themselves be seized by it only to tumble down the slopes of folly. They abandon the struggle because, even though the situation makes them suffer, they enjoy it in a masochistic psychopathological way.

The effort to persevere at lofty objectives is an achievement of the *awakened conscience*, objectives that lift individuals from intellectual and moral parasitism to the level where countless, dormant, inner resources bloom just waiting to be awakened by the will.

Like any other type of conditioning, perseverance is the result of the persistence individuals impose on themselves to achieve the objectives that promote and dignify them. There is no one devoid of perseverance or who is incapable of achieving it, because it results only from the desire that becomes an actual attempt, to be accomplished by continuous action.

From the acquisition of patience, and then perseverance – which completes it – one proceeds to self-confidence, i.e. to the certainty about existing possibilities that may be used for fulfilling one's inner longings. Fear vanishes, along with the self-punishing, self-afflicting mechanisms that disrupt the individual's evolution.

With self-confidence, the will is controlled by a healthy mind, which discerns what one should and can do, what one's objectives in life on earth are, and how to mature emotionally and psychologically to confront the vicissitudes, difficulties and problems that make up part of one's inner growth.

In this endeavor, the *psychological child*, sleeping within and insisting on being comforted, gives way to the adult with a firm and confident will, who plans his or her acts and works diligently to attain satisfactory results. In this undertaking, he or she does not desire to triumph over others, to conquer the world, to become famous, to lead the masses or to be deified, because this is a struggle for self-conquest, for inner realization, from whose efforts other *possessions* result, those of secondary importance, but which also make up part of the existential mechanisms that comprise development, the progress of society, the rise of its leaders, stars and builders of the future.

This whole enterprise is the result of a disciplined will, which becomes the best device in the victory of the thinking individual's physical existence on the earth.

Equipped with these three invaluable tools, a new cycle of maturation begins for human beings, who now aspire to conquering the universe because their inner cosmos is already under control.

LIBERATING ACTIONS

Possessing the skillful tools for disciplining the will, and thus upholding the knowledge of the Self, it is obvious that individuals self-awaken, perceiving their own reality and the objectives essential for enjoying a healthy life, although this does not imply living without any sort of afflictions or challenges. Rather, having acquired awareness of their own limits, they expand them into new possibilities for accomplishment, the same happening in relation to the normal phenomena that make up part of the evolutionary journey.

Thus considered, such individuals realize they must take action, for knowledge without actual, everyday experience does not yet mean actual balance, for its endurance will not have been tested.

The moment has arrived on the earth to unveil what had been hidden. This is not to say that this phase is to be worse than those that have passed. Actually, it is characterized by many blessings resulting from the progress and cultural development of its inhabitants, even though there are still many evolutionary misfortunes in the form of violence, of disregard for the sovereign laws of Life, of chaos – all as serious as they are perturbing.

There are many moral mishaps that come to public awareness and delight the tabloids and the general media. People take an interest in them because they are unconscious projections of what is engraved within them but lies hidden. For some reason, people take pleasure in other people's misfortunes. They see themselves reflected in others who might seem noble and good, but who actually bear the same miseries. Consequently, they love to divulge the mishap – hypocritically at times – giving the impression of feeling sorry, when, in fact, they are actually gloating while spreading gossip. Or they may rise up and attack, in the name of morality or the defense of higher ideals, acting angry because others have managed to do what they themselves would like to have done but could not, because they did not have enough *courage*, or because the circumstances were unfavorable.

Emotional behavior is far too complex to be reduced to patterns that inspire safety and structure. This is due to individuals' evolution through many reincarnations, where their multi-millenary periods of experience at the earliest levels of development predominate, in relation to their *short amount of time* in the realm of reason, discernment and love.

Actions, therefore, are the reflection of the fixation of psychological and intellectual achievements, becoming realities on the stage of human behavior and personal interrelationships.

They begin as tolerance toward those on the lower levels of moral growth, providing them with fraternal opportunities for self-realization, while at the same time helping them directly with their inner and outer growth.

True tolerance is an invaluable achievement that becomes a degree of progress because it encourages new expressions of solidarity, accentuating unrestricted forgiveness of all harm that has been done, with real forgetfulness of the offense.

Overcoming this challenge is a major step forward on the road to personal illumination, which opens the way for deeds of fraternal charity, of assisting the neediest, of being present wherever support and help are indispensable.

Action is the word of order throughout the universe. Movement is the mechanism that drives life in all directions.

Human beings only identify themselves with their reality when they act and become useful, detached from material things and still-primitive personal passions. Many of their misfortunes are life lessons, whose moral message they must understand and store. Unexpected infirmities, unpleasant events, premature deaths, surprising separations, and being unjustly accused are occurrences that solidify and ennoble a spirit's character, promoting it from lower mental wavebands to higher ones, which ensue in the process of liberation.

Therefore, not every misfortune is to be lamented, but accepted positively. Life knows what is necessary for individuals, providing for them according to their ability to accept and the opportunity to experience.

This way, self-awakened individuals cannot postpone their contribution to their social environment and they begin to act tirelessly.

Their actions become a preponderant factor for the progress of all other individuals, who are now their brothers and sisters on the same journey.

Their ascension raises others in turn; their fall leads others into the abyss. Their responsibility becomes significant, since, self-aware of their commitments, they understand why they are currently on the earth, and they know how to disencumber themselves from confrontations and struggles, preserving their moral and humane values.

Any conflicts that might arise are no longer a cause of imbalance or perturbation, but an opportunity to broaden their ability to understand and solve, to grow infinitely, because their future is the full attainment of the Self, overcoming all the obstacles that result from past incarnations, with a view to reaching the challenging propositions of the future.

9
HEALTHY RELATIONSHIPS

*The Influence of Myths on the Formation
of the Personality. Mistaken and Perturbing
Concepts. Behavioral Stability.*

HEALTHY RELATIONSHIPS

Human beings cannot live without the harmony of their social group. *Gregarious animals*, they are nourished by the energy and presence of others like them, who stimulate them to advance in their quest for self-realization.

The social relationship is of major importance for developing the qualities that lie sleeping in the folds of the unconscious, awaiting stimuli to bring them to the surface. This is possible only by living with other individuals of the same ilk.

Wanting to be alone all the time is a symptom of emotional maladjustment, and thus a psychopathology requiring proper treatment.

As they live with others, human beings smooth out their rough inner edges and adapt to their group. They learn that complete attunement to others results in productivity and the moral growth of society. Their own growth is growth for everybody; their failure is a collective failure. In this endeavor, therefore, they discover the beauty of harmony, which is the result of complete oneness with everyone else in the group.

Those who doubt the value of self-denial for the good of the social group should imagine what would happen to an orchestra in which one instrument decides to stand out, breaking away from the original score. It would obviously compromise the endeavor of the whole.

Thus, there is an ethical, psychological and moral need for relationships, especially healthy ones. Their purpose arises from fraternal interaction, cultural aspirations and praiseworthy contributions that make for enriching exchanges.

Human stimuli function in accordance with the purposes in mind. The mind, working the brain's neurons, stimulates the production of enzymes suitable either for sentiments of solidarity or bellicose reactions. Hence, aspiring to and maintaining lofty ideals is the best means for forming healthy relationships.

THE INFLUENCE OF MYTHS ON THE FORMATION OF THE PERSONALITY

All individuals are natural heirs of their past lives. Anthropological evolution remains imprinted on the panels of the deep unconscious, on the spirit itself, which becomes socialized and unfolds its mental potential through successive, uninterrupted lifetimes, something that enables it to grow and acquire a greater sum of intellectual-moral values.

Thus, myths lie at the core of their formation and make up an integral part of their current behavior. Various levels of attitudes and accomplishments, longings and plans rest, unconscious, on myths that have not been decoded by the conscious. The *fear of God*, left over from *primitive thought*, automatically continues to lead individuals to religious expressions that have no logical structure whatsoever. This is an instinctive attempt at Self-preservation, should a Higher Being, Creator of the universe, actually exist. As a consequence, social behavior continues to be characterized by threats, impositions, and unreasonable and anthological demands, disguising the fear that continues to control them in the fibers of their misdirected sentiments.

Not having been able to overcome the infantile, inner impressions that have remained in the form of unjustifiable attitudes, individuals continue to make their lives a proscenium dedicated to living out their inner dramas and conflicts, hoping for applause from the surrounding audience. Unaware of everyday reality, they flee to the scenery of the fables that enchanted their childhood and wait for the fantastic presences that will remove the oppressive burden of work, effort and cultural accomplishment, electing them as privileged and semi-divine. Consequently, their personality undergoes constitutive deformation and manifests with signs of morbidity.

As individuals evolve psychologically, myths, as archetypes, undergo transformation and adaptation to the dynamics of the different periods of growth and maturation. Fantasies are replaced with new, realistic aspirations, which fuse into the imagination, freeing up space for balanced and healthy development.

At the root of many bizarre behaviors, one may find undiluted myths controlling still-immature individuals.

Many of these myths originated in events that could not be verified and thus they entered the gallery of the imagination, enriched by the dreams and aspirations of successive persons and generations, who gave them real life at times, but only a symbolic character at others.

Peoples and civilizations that might have existed, such as the *Atlanteans* and *Lemurians*, entered that gallery of myths, some of which found their way into various *sacred books*, describing the creation of human beings, their expulsion from paradise, the flood, Noah's ark, and the alliance between God and humans. Later, they were reborn in the wonderful fables of India, China, Tibet, and Japan, and in the gods of the great civilizations of North Africa and the Middle East, or in the West, in the Greco-Roman pantheon with the rise of god-humans and human-gods, with passions and sublimations that were passed down from generation to generation to modern humans, somewhat molding their personalities.

Liberation from myths becomes possible when individuals acquire enough moral and cultural character to confront and de-mythify themselves, resolving to assume their own spiritual reality.

Human existence, however, plays out in a world marked by conflicts, ruthless competition, and disrespect for true human values, thus pushing the weakest psychological constitutions toward fantasy, to occasional flights from objective reality, where they seek refuge and protection in the imagination, emotionally stagnating or regressing to childhood. Phobias, insecurity and timidity manifest in their attitudes, which result from fear of a culture of aggression and disregard by the apparent winners.

Moreover, religious imagination has helped preserve such myths, bearers of special gifts and favors that are bestowed upon the elect, or those who force their way amongst the elect, using the same means with which the powerful on earth conquer one another, keeping supplicants in a state of dependency, with no opportunity for inner growth.

This case entails *gnomes, fairies and angels*, possessed of the ingredients for fertile imaginations that make them out to be special beings, bearers of unimaginable power and inexhaustible resources, which they put at the disposal of their followers, all those who submit to and worship them. Fantasies thrive and excesses seduce the incautious, who abandon reason to take part in the marketplace of illusion, submitting to impositions that do not advance them from either the psychological or cultural point of view.

Possessing one of these personifications – which represent archetypical images of ancient phobias and aspirations – offers strength and power to individuals to overcome bad luck, daily problems or suffering, and to live in a privileged manner within the social group without having to endure the natural injunctions of inner growth.

It would be strange enough if one found this quasi-fetishist cult only amongst uneducated persons. However, it is present and disseminated amongst all social segments because reincarnate spirits come from ancient cults, and they are still marked by impressionable atavisms from the primitive period of thought.

By eliminating creation myths, Spiritist psychology offers a scientific vision of the facts. It stimulates inner growth without fear or prejudicial constrictions on reason. Reality without crudity, objectivism without magic, subjectivism without superstition show that attaining happiness and personal harmony depend on the efforts each individual puts forth to be free, to aspire to the future, in order to soar, not by using the imagination, but by using the resources of the psyche, toward Cosmic Consciousness, which develops within, little by little.

MISTAKEN AND PERTURBING CONCEPTS

Psychologically immature, human beings suffer the anguish of uncertainty about their conduct within their social group. This insecurity often leads them to dubious behaviors that lack any equalizing meaning. Since they feel unable to express their own reality, they try to please everyone else, thus suffocating their own aspirations and adopting attitudes that are contrary to who they really are. They become a mirror that reflects other people, losing their own identity and slipping into conflicts that become more and more disquieting. Believing that this might be a way to receive social and emotional support, they act out of character and end up not really experiencing the success they were hoping for, because people are highly complex and insecure, and what pleases them at one moment might not please them the next. Relationships degenerate and suspicions replace the trust that once existed, wearing down both parties.

In this situation, individuals take on an aggressive attitude by showing their true colors and, refusing to tone down their insecurity and disappointment, they become a disagreeable presence in their social environment, which expects as many valuable contributions as possible, resulting in overall well-being and harmony.

Such individuals do not really know what they want, where they are headed or how to behave, for they are in a somnambulistic state, which has *flashes* of lucidity but soon returns to numbness.

Since they are so concerned about others, they forget themselves, disparaging themselves or being aggressive, whereas they should simply awaken to their own reality and that of their environment. However, they become robot-like in their torpor and let themselves be led by the rules imposed on them, even though these do not meet their personal demands and needs; or they follow traditions that are irrelevant to their objectives, affected by conditionings that are the results of previous inheritances that have no connection with their way of being. Thus, they let themselves be influenced by the sensationalism of mass media or suffocated by their social group.

They would like to be active members of their group, which rejects them, or they exile themselves by not grasping their existential role. Real awakening thus becomes indispensable for them by reflecting on their own aspirations and what is happening around them, so they may be at peace within the human context and be free, without narcissistic exhibitionism or depressive timidity.

The Apostle Paul, acting as a psychotherapist upon observing the lethargy in those around him – also characteristic of our own times – proclaimed in Ephesians 5:14 (which we have already referred to): *"Wake up, you who sleep, rise from the dead, and Christ will shine on you!"*

Sleep produces the death of reason, lucidity and the lofty commitment to the Self, and since Christ means discernment, a life's purpose and knowledge, it is necessary to become one with Him in order to live in clarity and be always awake to life.

The process of liberation imposes a few invaluable requisites, such as: asking oneself what one really wants out of the physical existence, what to do to identify with one's objectives, and if one's actions will lead to one's hoped-for goals. It is a resolute undertaking that must not be subjected to mood swings or to uncertainties created by insecurity. Once the goal is set, one must pursue it and live with the consequences, because the price of every lofty ideal is effort and dedication, an onus of sacrifice.

Breaking free of the psychological *crutch* of support during difficulties is a decisive step on the way to victory.

Likewise, life requires individuals to break free of self-pity, which is a way to call attention to themselves. People then regard them as needy and therefore lacking affection.

The real world has no room for compassion in the molds of conventional pity, which is not constructive, nor is it dignifying to anyone. In the great battle, in order for the strongest to survive – a rule of nature itself – the weak, the timid, the insecure, the childish and the self-pitying remain on the sidelines of progress, cultivating their limitations as the train of evolution continues up the mountain.

Individuals have no reason for self-pity. Such paranoid behavior is unjustified and results from the acceptance of one's own fragility, which strives to prolong one's dependence on others, something very convenient in the arena of moral challenges. This erroneous concept of waiting for others to help them, solely because they come across as weak, has no place in wholesome individuals, who use their lucidity to confront vicissitudes that develop their ability to face challenges and future undertakings.

Individuals make themselves strong because they have an inner strength that is waiting for the opportunity to bloom. Their emotional charge must be conducted and released as circumstances allow, storing up the resources of realization and growth, which are within everyone's reach.

In human relationships, only those that offer security and happiness provide renewal and enthusiasm to conscious individuals.

Pondering what one is and what one appears to be is a means of asserting one's identity and breaking free from the mechanisms of evading reality.

BEHAVIORAL STABILITY

Healthy behavior follows a balanced direction, without the constant ups and downs of the neurotic disorders that produce emotional instability. The range of values acquires integrity and takes control of one's attitudes as much as possible.

Such individuals remain awake, alert to their responsibilities on the scene of human accomplishments, and they are not marked by the uncertainties and limitations that used to characterize them. There is a lucid integration with the commitments they assume and they have positive relationships with everyone, the result of self-esteem and the affection for others. No longer enclosed within the shell of the ego, they see the world rightly. They comprehend its rules, but more importantly, they realize that they are eternal beings, whose trajectory on the earth has a higher purpose: the acquisition of latent resources, their divine inheritance awaiting development.

Their behavioral stability is not dependent on intentionally established rules, but is the result of inner maturity, which teaches them how to act regarding everyday challenges, how to confront situations that are less than favorable, how to perceive the meaning of events, and how to let themselves be filled with qualities resulting from their emotional maturity.

They go through times of difficulty with the same ease with which they relish moments of joy. They seek to learn the lesson hidden in each experience, since each one bears a message that can contribute to perfecting the individual. Thus, theirs is an agreeable form of living, marked by self-identity and self-realization.

This does not imply an absence of struggle; on the contrary, they become stronger because the horizons that open up before them get broader and their plans for achievement are greater. Struggles arise as new challenges that create momentary doubt, confusion, and conflicts for qualitative selection... However, these imperatives are diluted relatively easily, giving way to discernment, which chooses what must and can be done, leaving no room for unnecessary afflictions that may perturb habitual behavior.

Tension, a component of the human struggle, does not cause them stress. It is temporary and is quickly replaced by balance and confidence is one's ability to confront problems and solve them constructively.

Such behaviorally stable individuals display moral qualities that make them men and women of the good, bearers of remarkable inner accomplishments, individuals that do not get confused or perturbed by life's hard knocks.

These persons of the good are lucid because they know their limitations, but they also know their infinite potential for growth and so they plunge into the task of reaching for new heights.

They are not intimidated by the call to perfection because they are used to all kinds of accomplishments, having surpassed their inner limits and the external barriers of conventionalism, inherited myths and unjustifiable suspicions. They have become an active part of the universal whole with the kind of harmonious personal performance that provides the joy of living.

10
THE SEARCH FOR REALITY

Human Needs.
Conflicting Struggles. Self-Realization.

D ue to their atavisms and sleeping consciousness, human beings do not know how to choose what is fundamental for their transitory existence in the world or for their reality as immortal beings. They act through automatisms in the search for pleasure and although they do dare to pursue liberating experiences, they do not do so wholeheartedly, even though it should be the essential object of their reincarnation.

Imprisoned within the body, which acts as a kind of armor for developing their moral qualities while on the earth, it is difficult for them to exercise the higher emotions that could provide them with mental balance, and consequently much physical well-being, even during times of infirmity, which are meant to cleanse their biological organization.

In the physical world, form is always in transformation, so it is inevitable that infirmity and decay afflict the physical body with their unpleasant sensations of pain and dissatisfaction. Nevertheless, if human beings manage to harmonize with the cosmos – through perfect attunement between the Self and the Infinite – they can overcome such brief constrictions and experience the lofty manifestations of inner bliss, modifying their usual axiological level and beginning to value that which is long-lasting, beckoning to them with the designs of immortality. This is not just some theoretical vision. Survival after molecular destruction is a fact that drives individuals to internalize relevant personal accomplishments so that they can develop their behavior according to a judicious and lucid plan entailing definite objectives that may be reached in a conscious manner.

This reality must be pursued as a basic need for their evolution, which, due to the very transient nature of the physical body, must not be put off *sine die*.

HUMAN NEEDS

Human beings have set needs that are proper for their lives. These entail the whole gamut of physiological phenomena: food, shelter, clothing, safety, reproduction, well-being and social position. We may designate such needs as immediate or secondary from the psychological and ethical-esthetic points of view. Inevitably, meeting such needs does not wholly fulfill human beings, and other needs of a superior nature arise that are independent of those of immediate, palpable content: beauty, harmony, knowledge, art, religion and spiritual surrender.

The whole of anthropological inheritance is rooted in the basic automatisms of physical survival; in the struggle with other species; in foresight by storing up goods that will ensure the continuation of life; in procreation and the defense of offspring and property... To guarantee such things, humans have become bellicose and distrustful, and have developed the preservation instinct, from the sharpening of their sense of smell to the intuitive perception of danger.

Since these basic, indispensable needs are designed as part of their inner world, humans are involved in an ongoing struggle, often weaved of endless suffering because they lack reflection and the ability to distinguish between what is essential and what is superfluous.

Imprisoned within the small circle of such needs, even as they become more educated, their level of values remains the same, not having really transformed their objectives and achievements. All of their accomplishments may be summed up in the physiological, *inferior* principles of immediate results and fleeting significance.

When everything is in place and abundant, they fall prey to the fear of loss, of being usurped, and they dive headlong into the craze of wanting for more and more, so as to be protected against the so-called uncertainties of fate and life. If they experience lack, because they have not amassed as much as they would have liked in order to feel safe and secure, they become anxious. This is due to their mistaken notion about life and its goals.

Of course, people cannot live without a minimum of material resources, a dignified, social and balanced existence. However, this minimum of resources is enough to meet and support other psychological, higher values, which place individuals above the oscillating circumstances of having and not having.

People's biggest concern should be how they handle the challenges of their own reality, which is not thought of as being essential for their self-identity and complete self-realization.

The daily struggle produces immediate results, which contribute to meeting the basic needs of existence, but it is essential that individuals branch out to meet other important evolutionary demands, those of a psychological nature, transcending place, situation, position and power.

While a full stomach may provide bodily satisfaction, an edifying conversation with a friend provides mental well-being; an estate filled with rare and expensive pieces may offer joy and comfort, but a moment of meditation enriches one with unparalleled inner peace; support from bodyguards or the authorities may, in many cases, provide security, but a clear conscience, which results from upright conduct, provides complete tranquility; an assortment of clothes may aid one's appearance, but mental harmony and kindness radiate uncommon beauty; sexual prowess may draw attention in social circles, but the ecstasy of one moment of profound love rewards, renews and revitalizes the individual; social status may massage the ego, but the attainment of the Self makes for inner bliss…

The basic physiological needs are always accompanied by more demands because they soon lose their function. Those of a higher psychological nature develop into countless variants, which never cease to provide beauty.

Therefore, individuals' reality goes beyond their looks and the clothes they wear. It is to be found in their intrinsic qualities, which deserve the full contribution of emotional and mental effort to manifest.

Only then does health become viable, the good asserts its presence, and the noble ideals of society and the individual become legitimate and easy to reach by all those who are committed to achieving them.

CONFLICTING STRUGGLES

To live is to struggle. In the remote past, the strongest defeated the weak and imposed their presence, opening the way for anthropological evolution. As the brain developed under the influence of the spirit, thereby becoming increasingly complex, intelligence contributed to making the process less aggressive, although a number of animal-like manifestations still predominate in human beings. Though already able to tell right from wrong, they repeat bloody struggles due to atavism and a sense of cruelty – often pathological – that will slowly be overcome by the same force of evolution.

In spite of this, abandoning the most immediate levels of what may be regarded as a need for survival requires a struggle between what one enjoys and what one wants, what one has and what can and must be attained.

This struggle has much to do with ancestral habits that have left deep furrows in the unconscious, habits that are repeated almost automatically and must be overcome by reason. In this effort, feelings from recent reincarnations resurface. These feelings are characterized by the predominance of the instinct, without the dominant matrices of reason or the sentiment of solidarity. Thus, they resurface as inner torment, frustrations and shame, requiring appropriate therapy and personal effort to overcome limits imposed by the circumstances.

Just as there are phototropism and heliotropism, life entails a superior psychotropism that drives newly created beings to grow, to set a course for the Causal and Organizing Thought of all things. The attraction is unavoidable and no one can escape this commanding magnetism, which vitalizes and envelops everything.

The struggle is of an inward nature in individuals used to putting forth little effort of their own, while often exploiting other people's labor. Each person plays an important role in this endeavor to ascend; no one can fulfill another person's commitment. Growth is accomplished with sweat and well-directed effort, which makes it rewarding and fascinating in and of itself, opening up new opportunities and developing other venues of integration that are no longer in tune with self-pity, anguish or fear – limits to which they are accustomed. The evolutionary challenge is huge and all individuals are led unavoidably to meet it.

Since struggle can offer progressively better results because it strengthens the combatants, the struggle connected with evolving from basic to liberating needs will surpass all other conflicts and release individuals from the shackles that keep them from progressing.

Human beings who exist bearing the yoke of personal insecurity about life have acclimated themselves to the regions of darkness, where they find refuge to bemoan their rather self-serving limitations, afraid to make decisions that would liberate them, but which, on the other hand, demand resolve, sacrifice and the courage not to give up. Once this new battle to evolve further has begun, even in the face of conflict, the first step has already been taken, which soon leads to others, until the moment when the joy of freedom becomes the incentive for more daring accomplishments.

Let no one expect to win by counting on others to do the work on his or her behalf, since victory is personal and non-transferrable. There is no room for fraud or deceit.

When primitive humans raised their eyes to the Infinite, they became frightened and bowed down before its unfathomable majesty. Slowly, however, probing nature and overcoming their limitations, they went from basic to more refined instincts and opened the way for reason, which enabled them to reach the first manifestations of intuition, which will be human beings' future heritage, once they break completely free from the constraints of matter.

Thus, conflictive struggle gives way to conscious and rational struggle, for the goal becomes apparent. Without this victory suffering remains a dictator imposing its arbitrary and often unnecessary demands.

Life does not require pain; life offers love. Pain is a device for experiencing love, which has not always been appreciated as it should.

In this way, the mechanisms of evolution impose higher-level ethical, moral and esthetic needs, which will then foster even greater ones of a metaphysical nature, for they will probe life's highest realms for growth.

SELF-REALIZATION

Bearing in mind the imperative of their immediate, physiological needs as essential for preserving their body and activity within their social group, individuals should, nonetheless, give themselves room for those of an esthetic nature, that is, those that embellish life and act as a portico to *metaneeds*.

Men and women who are actually awake to their responsibilities go through the different stages of their basic needs free from attachments or imprisonments. They realize that cultural and artistic achievements, which offer them esthetic vision and fascination, also sensitize the emotional brain with the understanding and absorption of their contents through reason.

Once beyond this phase, they detect the *metaneeds*, which make loud appeals to self-discovery, to interiorization, through which they reach self-realization.

This process occurs slowly as the result of dissatisfaction with what has been accomplished thus far, causing a loss of motivation, empathy and meaning for continuing the struggle. At other times, metaneeds arise as insights opening up one's perceptions to transpersonal reality, which ceases to be an epiphenomenon of the central nervous system or a hallucination, to appear as an objective structure and become a reality.

Persons at this level of psychological growth meditate on their existential objectives and yearn for the continuation of life, which does not end with organic death.

Discovering the fact that they are a *bundle of energy* under the action and control of the thinking conscious, they grasp the weakness of materialism and immerse themselves in their inner ocean, liberating the *sacred unconscious*, which enables them to break free from their primitive remnants, because they ascend to the higher frequency of the causal regions of life and begin to attune to the living, acting forces of the Divine Thought.

They control the "organic machine" and its functions, and they manage to unravel themselves from their perispiritual ties and travel by means of the *psychonautical* vehicle, becoming exhilarated and vitalized in such a way that all their aspirations experience a shift and begin to focus on the real, authentic being, which is the spirit.

An intense joy invades these new, self-realized navigators.

Metaneeds become imperative, opening up broader, more attractive landscapes, which, when entered, bless with even more joy.

These individuals thus become their own therapists. They no longer tumble into their old habitual, ancestral turpitudes, for they have broken free from corrupting and harmful conditionings because they have aspired to and lived amongst other, enriching landscapes of a purer and more meaningful psychosphere.

After having returned from one such meta-excursion, the Apostle Paul stated emphatically: *Rejoice always!* (1 Thes. 5:16)

The psychotherapy he offers is concise and without further commentary as a must for immediate self-realization, without ostentation or uncalled-for justification.

He is not referring to rejoicing only in times of happiness and peace, but always and in any circumstance; living joyfully in difficult and trying times as well, knowing they are important for our liberation, which fully justifies them.

In an even deeper analysis, this imperative is extended to unpleasant, seemingly harmful events, such as those entailing physical and mental torment that leave damage and impairment, which are converted into renewal and a new beginning.

Thus, a *metaneed* clamors for a change in behavior, transforming bitterness into smiles, rebelliousness into selflessness, grief into forgiveness, disenchantment into hope, through which causes of perturbation are overcome and illuminative treasures won.

Climbing ascending steps, awakened individuals slit their inner darkness with the luminous dagger of self-realization. Using the techniques and resources of prayer, they dilute anxieties and conflicts. By focusing on their *metaneeds*, after having provided for their physiological and ethical-esthetic needs, they immerse themselves in meditation, from which they emerge to practice love, the good, and the liberation of lives.

This magnificent odyssey can and must be attempted at any stage of existence, even under the urge of physiological necessities, by choosing a *metaneed* and striving to meet it.

This attempt will leave furrows and fertile marks on the conscience, which will aspire to new accomplishments, creating the habit of self-nourishment with this vigorous soul energy that entices one to break free from basic and immediate primary needs.

Individuals advance from ignorance to knowledge, from the brutish form to the superior essence, self-realizing, living their own inherent immortality.

11
LIFE: CHALLENGES
AND SOLUTIONS

*The Intellectual Brain
and the Emotional Brain. Meditation and
Visualization. Well-Directed Thought.*

P hysical life is an illuminating experience faced with innumerable challenges throughout its course. Meeting these challenges requires well-directed effort.

Thanks to their gregarious instinct, human beings find it necessary to create social groups for their development. In the framework of the social group, individuals receive assistance and offer resources that are added to the contributions of the past so that life may be more pleasant and enriching. Nevertheless, due to their atavisms and aggressive attitudes, they suffer constricting injunctions that suffocate them with conflicts and torment them relentlessly. When they free themselves from one difficulty, they are usually confronted with another; driven to evolve, every step of the ascent demands sacrifice, selflessness and dedication.

Wherever they turn, they face calls to growth and to prove their faith amid frightening circumstances. If they are mature, they regard each victory as an evolutionary opportunity that will force them to face new challenges, as is the case with the phenomena of life itself, which causes different perceptions of reality, depending on the times. At each step there are values that are highly significant. As soon as one moves up to the next level, new values surface that stoke the interest of and require effort from the individual. However, if such individuals have not developed a certain level of self-discovery, of maturity, they are beset with complex dramas and lose themselves in the tangle of their passions and torments.

To live means to construct oneself inwardly, overcoming each level of evolution by means of self-improvement. This is no easy task, since it has a lot to do with individuals' moral and spiritual reality, for they are incessantly called to work on their self-worth, their inner growth, and to overcome belittling dependencies.

Impelled to external accomplishments, they have to deal with multiple perturbing emotional states: phobias, inferiority/superiority complexes, narcissism, egotism, resentment, anxiety about the future, lack of affection, various types of neuroses and psychoses – none of which they can manage, because they are not in the habit of going within to find out just exactly what they want out of life.

Comfortable with age-old habits, they fear self-discovery, using the excuse that they do not know how to confront themselves, since they have been running from their own reality the whole time.

At this stage, the problem-solving inner journey is urgent, without reserve, without rhetoric.

THE INTELLECTUAL BRAIN AND THE EMOTIONAL BRAIN

For 80 years, approximately, psychology was shackled to the concept of the *intellectual brain*, which was expressed in terms of IQ, the level of which indicated those who ought to succeed in life. All those who were intellectually gifted in some way were seen as examples of future success, leading to an almost arrogant attitude toward others, as if nothing more were needed for the happy life that everyone dreams of. Making use of the results of tests by Binet and Simon and their *metric scale of intelligence*, individuals' emotions were not taken into consideration. People were like robots that could confront problems and solve them in a cool, calculated manner, equipped as they were with an intelligence that could meet the most serious existential commitments.

A veritable *dictatorship* of high IQ levels selected types that were elect by nature, opening the doors of success to them, thereby creating a privileged caste that should direct human minds and society in general.

In practice, however, the results did not meet the expectations of its formulators. In fact, highly intelligent individuals do find it easier to solve the most serious challenges. However, there are other very important factors that need to be taken into consideration, such as those related to the *emotional brain*, because, before all else, humans are a bundle of emotions that guide, condition and develop plans for their psychological structure and contribute to their self-realization.

As time passed, it was possible to observe that super-gifted men and women could not achieve the success they desired due to their unwillingness to struggle, their inertia, or due to choosing other values-pleasures that made well-being difficult to achieve. On the other hand, less mentally endowed persons with IQs between 90 and 100 could become successful due to their tenacity and mental effort to reach the levels they promised to themselves, and because they did not stop struggling until they reached them. Quite often those with IQs of no more than 100 have guided those with IQs as high as 160...

Relationship and emotional skills are also fundamental for success.

Currently, psychology is facing a new approach regarding the development of *interpersonal* intelligence, which has to do with social relationships, the observation and monitoring of events, and the ability to discern, responding consciously to the various spiritual states, different temperaments, and care that must be used in the treatment of others, something that goes way beyond intellectual robotization.

Consequently, it is necessary to harmonize emotion and thought, such that they mutually aid each other, with emotion providing warmth to reason, which in turn offers understanding to the *heart*, thus avoiding remaining on just one aspect of the reality that makes up the human being.

Of course, misdirected emotions perturb one's thought, making concentration difficult and working against the intellect. In the same way, cold and logical intelligence creates obstacles to sharing, to emotional focus, rendering individuals deprived of love and sensitivity. They may express all the beauty, describe all the harmony, and speak of all the greatness of life, but will feel nothing, rendering it only intellectual and lifeless in form.

When emotions predominate, attitudes are embarrassing, and persons simply cannot think correctly or tell right from wrong, creating behavioral problems. *Neuroscience* says that this phenomenon is the result of the *functional memory*, located in the pre-frontal cortex. Hence, it is necessary that, in the festival of life, emotions coexist well with reason so that sentiment and thought contribute mutually to the commitment to happy results in human decisions and conduct.

We will conclude by saying that individuals have *two brains*: *the emotional* and *the rational*, which we may say are two types of intelligence, or even two types of minds. The development of both corresponds to the successes or failures that affect human beings.

MEDITATION AND VISUALIZATION

In order to live well and evolve properly, a profound self-analysis is indispensable for facing life's challenges and finding appropriate solutions.

Of all the many methods, we are of the opinion that meditation – without religious or sectarian elements, and more as a therapy than anything else – offers the best means for this profound incursion. Different schools use different methods and each one is more demanding than the next in relation to the details, for they are convinced of the excellence of their results. They merit our respect, but not our adoption for what we are proposing within the context of thought and self-identity.

Thus, posture, mantras or conditioning melodies are not what matter; what does matter are the means that are most compatible with each practitioner and his or her psychological endurance. It is always a good idea to have good breathing in mind as a way to eliminate the carbon dioxide that has remained in the lungs due to respiratory deficiency, and adopt a posture that does not make one feel heavy, tired or constricted. Next, one should choose what to meditate about and how to go about it.

Since our proposal is not related to the techniques of Transcendental Meditation or any of the other approaches known in Esotericism, Yoga, etc., we suggest that you try to relax a much as possible by beginning to concentrate on various parts of the body: the scalp, forehead, eyes (closed or open – whichever works better), face, on down to the toes.

Repeating this exercise will lead to new mental conditioning, inducing the thought to remain firm regarding its goals, and reasoning, which is its main characteristic.

In order to avoid becoming dependent on it, it would be best not to listen to music at first. Later, when acclimated to the experience, music may exert a therapeutic function, contributing to relaxation.

You should keep the time available in mind. At first, the endeavor should be brief, slowly increasing to what can be experienced comfortably and peacefully, finally reaching the desirable length of 30 to 60 minutes, depending on what is possible for you.

There are no set rules, but measures that facilitate educating the mind and create the habit of going within, despite the chaos in which one lives, far removed from anything that induces mental silence, balanced emotions and harmonious thought.

The mind is a *rebellious colt*, which must be brought under control by the effort of directing it toward values that elevate and dignify the individual. The polyvalence of worries, appeals and needs leaves it continuously agitated or exhausted and incapable of making further contributions when out-of-the-ordinary collaborations are asked of it. It finds it hard to concentrate and register different ideas.

Once a comfortable atmosphere of relaxation has been attained, breathe by inhaling with the mouth closed, holding the breath for a while with the mouth shut, and then exhaling through slightly opened lips. In this way, the habitual, conventional structure of breathing becomes modified, giving way to a new healthy method of absorbing and eliminating air.

Over the first few days of this exercise, as a result of right breathing you will notice an organic, muscular renewal and you will be in a better mood in relation to your activities. Then you should proceed to visualization, which is a way to enrich the thought and memory, ridding the latter of pessimistic, perturbing, habitual fixations.

All it takes is to think about a pleasant place: a peaceful beach, a fragrant forest, a colorful garden, a gentle, singing stream, a mirror-like lake, a lofty mountain, a lovely nook – any place that offers a landscape, an enchanting and comforting view – for you to go there mentally.

As you remain relaxed and continue to breathe, the mind, which prepares a place or memory that recalls an alluring reference point, such as a colorful picture, should hold on to it and experience the pleasant harmonies while it lets itself be imbued with the uncharted forces of nature, facilitating attunement with the omnipresent Divine Energy, clearing the way for influence by high-order spirits, who use such moments to help their wards, especially those interested in their own moral growth.

Once this new habit is set, you can visualize a pleasant event that has been stored in the unconscious and recall it via active memory to experience it again in such a way that it becomes vivid and healthy, providing the same well-being as it did the first time.

This procedure will help the emotions relive happy scenes, which *lie buried* under accumulated disenchantments and problems that comprise a very unpleasant and troubling emotional burden.

Using this simple method for reliving happy times, you may also visualize unpleasant moments, bad experiences, which have left caustic residues and serious resentment, pardoning and forgiving the offender, retrieving the files from the unconscious and becoming free to fill up the space with life-enhancing situations.

Lastly, visualize a great light with soft, penetrating tonalities, allowing it to enter via the coronary center, permeating the circulatory system, reaching the brain and the rest of the body, slowly freeing it from the harmful energies that facilitate the proliferation of destructive microorganisms and *mental larvae, thought-forms,* etc., which contribute to degenerative illnesses. Using the power of the mind, you can free up the impediments that the light may find in the arteries and veins until the entire body is a luminous torrent on the inside.

Remain in this state of inner, therapeutic clarity for 3 to 5 minutes, holding your thought on the healthy visualization before slowly and peacefully returning to outer awareness.

It is obvious that you must choose a place where you can meditate and visualize, such that there are no worries, obstacles or disturbances.

When you have finished, hold on to the experience as naturally as possible on the mental screen until other concerns take its place without causing affliction.

With this simple technique, we have introduced a therapeutic form for releasing some of your conflicts, which should be brought, one by one, to visualization over time, overcoming and diluting them. In case there are a few that are hard to break free from, it is obvious that you need a support group or a certified psychotherapist.

Transpersonal psychology's view of individuals favors them with unimaginable potential for self-discovery, for self-realization attained with effort and good actions that can restore the moral credits that past life attitudes have wasted, causing damaging effects in the current incarnation.

Since individuals are on the earth to be happy and to overcome impediments to the perfection for which they are destined, every moral effort contributes to harmony and happiness.

Well-Directed Thought

Thought is a living, active force because it proceeds from the mind, which has its seat in the spirit; hence, it is the exteriorization of the eternal Entity.

Thought materializes in the world of form according to the way it is directed. Educating it is highly important since it is an essential means for confronting challenges and finding the solutions needed for a healthy life.

Normally, due to bad thought habits, individuals state that everything they think negatively about happens to them. They do not realize that they themselves are responsible for mentally constructing what they unconsciously long for and prepare through thought. If they would just alter the way they look at life and the way they think, everything would change, rendering their existence more satisfying and positive.

Neurolinguistics has shown that mental fixations contribute to human accomplishments, and *neuroscience* has confirmed the power of mental force in human activities.

It is a bad habit to cultivate destructive, pejorative, troubling thoughts because emitting them will create factors that facilitate their condensation in the emotional and physical arenas.

Every time one thinks about something unpleasant that is expected to happen and it actually does, it is time to change the way one formulates ideas, constructing them in an edifying and positive manner. Then, one will see that events change, becoming happier and more comforting.

We do not mean to say that the mere fact of developing an idea, what one wants or plans for will necessarily happen. Nevertheless, the mental wave will act as a propitiatory factor, which will contribute to rendering the desire viable. In addition, one must not fail to invest effort and intent so as to make it real, constructive and edifying.

Leaning towards masochistic tendencies, human beings – who love calling attention to themselves through pity instead of sound moral, intellectual, cultural, social, etc., values – always fixate on grievous complexes, mentally cultivating attitudes that generate unhappiness, thus developing a huge capacity for producing the desired effects.

Modifying their psychological structure by cleansing the conflict to which they cling, they must direct their mental force toward self-realization so that special factors may surface that help them change their inner landscape and outer occurrences, programmed as they are by the Divine Mind to reach Life's highest levels.

They must set their sights on the higher realms, so that growth occurs naturally, characterized by the blessings of joy, health and bliss.

The harmony prevailing in the universe is also found in human beings, who are presently developing such wonders that sing far and wide, stimulating them to evolve without repose, to work without fatigue, to do their best at all times. As such, existential challenges are part of life. Without them, individuals would be destroyed by the paralysis of the will, limbs and aspirations, which would be transformed into the unhealthy acceptance of the lowest rungs on the ladder of evolution.

Staying on course to the unconscious in order to free it from its primitive inheritances, and enriching the Self with the light of elevated discernment in an uninterrupted effort of self-growth and attunement to Life is the chief aim of reincarnation, which releases the spirit from the automatic wheel of *comings-and-goings* without accomplishments in accord with God's purposes. And since such conquest of the Infinite never stops – once one phase is finished, another, more challenging one appears – through such victories the spirit achieves plenitude and becomes *one with God*.

49915122R00095

Made in the USA
Columbia, SC
29 January 2019